Celtic Goddesses
and Their Spells

Celtic Goddesses and Their Spells

DISCOVER YOUR INNER GODDESS
THROUGH THESE AMAZING DIVINITIES

Gillian Kemp

Illustrations by Julia Cellini

CICO BOOKS

LONDON NEW YORK

Dedicated to Lynette Swift, Alison Kemp, and Helen Swift

Published in 2023 by CICO Books
An imprint of Ryland Peters & Small Ltd
20–21 Jockey's Fields   341 E 116th St
London WC1R 4BW   New York, NY 10029

www.rylandpeters.com

A version of this text was first published in 2022 as part of
The Celtic Goddess Oracle Deck

10 9 8 7 6 5 4 3 2 1

Text © Gillian Kemp 2023
Design © CICO Books 2023
Illustrations © Julia Cellini 2022, 2023

A CIP catalog record for this book is available from the
Library of Congress and the British Library.

ISBN: 978-1-80065-237-8

Printed in China

Senior designer: Emily Breen
Art director: Sally Powell
Creative director: Leslie Harrington
Head of production: Patricia Harrington
Publishing manager: Penny Craig

SAFETY NOTE
Never leave burning candles unattended

MIX
Paper from
responsible sources
FSC® C106563
FSC
www.fsc.org

Contents

INTRODUCTION 6
GODDESSES 10
INDEX 143

Introduction

All females are divinely attuned to goddesses from birth for guidance and protection through life until death. Working by divine plan, goddesses imbue us with their ancient wisdom, which becomes our own, helping us to avoid pitfalls and reach our full potential. Goddesses and druids were once humans and many places in the British Isles are named after them. Now these legendary beings are heavenly spirits who have personal relationships with you in everything you do. During your lifetime, goddesses come to help you when you ask them to. Goddesses have the same emotions as you. They know you deserve love, respect, kindness, and help. They have experienced all aspects of life that you have experienced or may encounter in the future. They always look after you kindly; no entreaty is too small or great, and they will never mock you or make you feel ashamed.

HOW GODDESSES CAN HELP

Goddesses hold treasured mysterious secrets, stored deep within our feminine intuition. This powerful book allows us to call goddesses into our world for inspirational divine intervention to help steer us on our path through life.

By embracing the magical blessings the goddesses bestow, we can connect with the very best of all our talents. Goddesses are maternal, sympathetic teachers and healers who offer wise guidance that awakens our feminine intuition and reveals our future to us. They help and empower us in a feminine way, much as our mothers, sisters, daughters, grandmothers, aunts, and female friends might.

If there is something personal you need advice on, or a particular issue you may be embarrassed to share, know that goddesses will never divulge your secrets. For prediction, guidance, empathy, affirmation, and strengthening of feminine intuition, goddesses love bestowing their help. Tell the goddesses your problems and you will be passing your worries on to a higher force to deal with on your behalf. You will feel relieved of your concern and imbued with peace of mind and omniscience, a seed of all-knowing. With divine intervention shining light on the situation, the issue will be resolved; working together with the goddesses, you can reach a resolution.

COMFORT AND GUIDANCE

With omniscient kindness, goddesses offer comfort in all key aspects of life, as well as in smaller, more insignificant things. Goddesses will inspire you with the wisdom to see life from a higher perspective and to feel a deeper understanding of your place in the world. They deliver security, comfort, and confidence, enabling you to believe in yourself and feel more optimistic and protected.

Alongside your existing religion, goddesses offer encouragement and insight into your path in life. They support you in retaining and developing what is good, and address potential self-wreckage from deficiencies and weaknesses that could detract from a fulfilling, happy life. The more you thank the goddesses, the more they will help you. They will also channel their powers through you to help others. Similarly, by means of divine behavior, goddesses will also work through other people to intervene in your life and influence events in it. The Ancient Egyptian word for this was *heka*, which translates as "magic."

The goddesses reward your faith in them. You will sense them working behind the scenes, intuitively feeling them communicating with you, nudging the jigsaw pieces of your life into place. Every time you light a candle, a goddess will draw close to you, attracted to the light.

You may also see and sense goddesses in nature. They will engineer situations so that you are in the right place, at the right time, with the right people. You are more receptive to goddesses when you are happy, because your vibration is lighter, and all goddesses are light. Goddesses rebalance your life, so if you've been going through a hard time they will repay you with the opposite, so you don't lose the essence of who you are.

Above all, they teach you to trust in your own intuition. If advice you have been given by someone does not sound, look, or feel right, or sit comfortably with you, then you are probably correct. Listen to your gut feeling, so you can make the right choice about what to say or do. This is what the goddesses teach you—to empower yourself from within. The more you trust your feminine intuition, the stronger the goddesses' power over your good fortune in life will be. The following pages will describe what each goddess represents, and what it may mean to sense their presence nearby.

This is what the goddesses teach you–
to empower yourself from within.

THE GODDESSES

Dana 12

Arianrhod 14

Elen 17

Coventina 19

Brigit 22

Branwen 25

Aimend 27

Scathach 30

Cliodna 32

Cred 35

Modron 37

Anu 40

Ban-Chuideachaidh
  Moire 42

Rosmerta 45

Adsullata 47

Latiaran 50

Cerridwen 52

Druantia 55

Andraste 57

Cessair 60

Flidais 62

Morgan le Fay 65

Guinevere 67

Caolainn 70

Ragnall 72

Cailleach 75

Igraine 77

Enid 80

Marcia Proba 82

Aerten 85

Maeve 87

Iseult 90

Awen 92

Dindrain 95

Nimue 97

Kundry 100

Eostre 102

Rhiannon 105

Habetrot 107

Aine 110

Turrean 112

Morrigan 115

Banba 118

Emer 120

Fand 123

Epona 125

Blodeuwedd 128

Cyhiraeth 130

Bo-Dhu 133

Sequana 135

Nair 138

Cethlenn 140

Dana

GODDESS OF EMPOWERMENT

KEYWORDS: Emboldened • Strengthened • Enriched

COUNTRY OF ORIGIN: Ireland

Dana presides over Lughnasadh (July 31), the beginning of the harvest season. Her name means "knowledge" and "to run, to flow." Married to Bile, god of light and healing, Dana was a divinatory healer of mothers, humans, animals, and broken people, to whom she taught self-worth. An undefeated warrior and mother of all the gods and Ireland, it's thought that Ireland's famous mists are her embrace, suggesting a state of flux before everything becomes clear and visible. In a difficult situation, clarity will come when you decide to do and say what feels correct. The knowledge and wisdom you gain will bring freedom and security, just as Dana's key opens and locks doors. You are closing the door on harmful and negative things, and opening it to self-discovery and empowerment. You are unlocking a door to your life's purpose by finding what makes you feel most happy and alive. This purpose gives your life direction and energy, which you channel from the cosmos since you are aligned with the universe.

Your self-confidence is growing as you need the approval of others less and won't let them steal your peace of mind. You love yourself and feel lighter and happier. You're rising above past mistakes and current problems and won't let other people undermine you. Even negative circumstances can boost your self-confidence, while encouraging other people's confidence empowers you, too. As a warrior and healer, Dana taught that the fear of losing should not be an obstacle to the elation of winning. Counteract negative thoughts undermining your power with a positive thought.

Dana has many symbols, including seagulls. Her seagulls show that you can defend your territory and live without fear. Like a persistent seagull searching for food, you'll find the right people to fulfill your needs and empower you to improve yourself, your circumstances, and your environment. Like a seagull traveling long distances, you'll extend your comfort zone and face challenges, and you'll soon visit the coast or plan a vacation overseas. Like seagulls who mate for life, you'll meet your lifelong partner if you haven't already done so.

In the same way that Dana stands beside a flowing river, so you move closer to your destination and the fulfillment of your needs. Your future success should not go to your head; it is heaven-sent to flow through you. Blessings from heaven, like the rain that fills rivers, empower you in a situation in which you've been faithful, true, and respectful. You're more powerful and needed than you might believe.

DANA'S MESSAGE Something wonderful will happen to make you feel on top of the world. It could involve love, family, career, or money. Dana's key signifies that your empowerment is key to this success— it will close the door on self-sabotage and open one to happiness. Your power increases as you take control, recognize your needs, and set new goals.

What you have been hoping to happen is now within your grasp—you can sense it and will see it come to fruition. By rising above your fears and negativity, you are realizing your true self-worth. Fortuitous events arriving through divine power will redouble and reinforce your prosperity and empowerment.

DANA'S SPELL FOR EMPOWERMENT Write a list of the things you want to achieve, short-term, long-term, or both. Take as many votive candles as the number of ambitions on your list and place them in a circle. Beginning clockwise, light the first candle and say the first item on your list. Light the second candle and say the second goal. Continue in this way until all the candles are lit and each listed thing has been said. Sit with the candles and absorb their light while saying: *"I am empowered to succeed in my plans."* Let the candles burn out. Keep the piece of paper in a clean, white envelope with your personal belongings and read the mantra as many times a week as you wish.

Arianrhod

GODDESS OF GOOD FORTUNE

KEYWORDS: Benevolence • Adaptability • New cycle

COUNTRY OF ORIGIN: Wales

Arianrhod is the goddess of good fortune. Holding a globe, it's thought she presides over the revolving year and evolution in the four seasons of your life. A provident provider and preserver of good luck, Arianrhod symbolizes that you're blessed with good fortune through life's unknowns. In every situation, you'll see divine intervention helping to resolve your problems. Misfortune, like good fortune, is fickle and never lasts forever, and divine intervention will not desert you as your fortunes change. Your strength of character will endure, which has a lot to do with luck rather than chance happenings. You're coming out of a phase of bad luck into a cycle of good luck with what was once difficult becoming easy.

Arianrhod, a servant of God's will, has two faces, indicating that people can invite bad luck by lacking the high-mindedness that changes bad luck to good. Good fortune reigns over only one half of your fate; the other is ruled by your free will and choices. Chance decides who gets good or bad luck, but luck can change to its opposite depending on your actions. Your spiritual body often grows when things go wrong and good luck can even come from misfortune. One sometimes depends on the death of the other to evolve your personality and position. The wheel carved into Arianrhod's chair alludes to you adapting to fate's ups and downs by anticipating the cyclic turning points. Your growth toward inner enlightenment and harmony evolves like a turning karmic wheel of cause and effect.

Good luck will always come to you because you deserve it. The cornucopia resting in Arianrhod's lap confirms that you'll be bestowed with financial prosperity and abundance. The ship's rudder above her chair means higher forces control and steer your fate. However, you also have control if you discern all influences that cross your path, while doing your best to keep on course.

Arianrhod is the personification of chance and using strength of character when circumstances call for this. Life would stagnate without change. New circumstances require adaptability, courage, and awareness to maintain balance. You control how you react and can see good from evil. Being visionary, many will confide in you for predictions of the future. Arianrhod was oracular and consulted daily. You may be helping your father, or a male relative, boss, co-worker, neighbor, or friend who you need to take control of on your terms.

A turn of events means you will make an important decision, empowering you to move toward fulfillment and freedom from restraints.

Arianrhod is the bearer of prosperity and increases the fruits of the Earth and female fertility.

Bountiful opportunities beckon in love, work, and wealth. Lady Luck is smiling on you. Imminent good events bring a long-lasting phase of good fortune, replacing the misfortune you've had tenfold. You're ready to use your talents and push yourself forward. You know what you want and will get it by using good fortune wisely to secure your future in your charmed wheel of life.

Arianrhod's crown of flowers is a reminder that honors are eternal, but fade, so must be renewed after every ending. Your individual, immortal soul continues through every emotional, physical, spiritual, or material test in life.

ARIANRHOD'S MESSAGE Push your luck and work so these don't push you. Your efforts will be rewarded as Arianrhod is the bearer of prosperity and increases the fruits of the Earth and female fertility. You are inspired to have the foresight to see ahead and the wisdom to know how to handle Lady Luck.

ARIANRHOD'S SPELL FOR LADY LUCK TO SMILE ON YOU Light a yellow candle to represent the sun. Write a list of what you would like to have in life and a separate list of what you wish to eliminate. Hold the lists in front of a mirror beside the candle while saying: *"Lady Luck, please smile on me; reflect all the luck I wish for to come to me."* Burn the piece of paper in the flame and allow the lists to reduce to ash in a dish. Snuff out the candle and bury the ash.

Elen

GODDESS OF DECISIONS

KEYWORDS: Victorious • Intelligence • Riches

COUNTRY OF ORIGIN: England

Queen of the night and witches, Elen presides over Hallowe'en (October 31), the holy evening when spirits roam the Earth, fall ends, and winter begins, like shed deer antlers that regrow yearly. Elen is also the goddess of crossroads. Three positive new paths are opening for you, all taking you in different directions. Each path will be of great significance, leading you to new people, feelings, and lifestyle. Elen helps prevent mistakes caused by spur-of-the-moment decisions and her intervention rectifies wrong choices. If you feel you're on a road to nowhere or have taken a wrong turn, follow your intuitive compass and change direction. There is always more than one way around a problem.

Relationships are on the road to recovery. People are now respecting your right of way, so a difficulty turns out to be more promising than you dared hope, bringing you a sense of achievement and setting your heart at rest. You have the means to carry out a task. With enthusiasm and energy, a dilemma that you may feel is hopeless will bring you cheer when you persevere.

Like the flickering flames of Elen's torch, emblematic of truth and divine wisdom spreading light, you'll bring things to life around you by getting the go-ahead for something you have been waiting for. Light guides and protects when your character is tested, igniting a germ of your spirituality, awakening optimism, determination, and a belief that events will bring you to where you want to be. The timing might be different to what you'd intended, but it will still be right.

The motion of Elen's flame is a heavenward channel of all supernatural universal powers bringing you the instant power of spirit, knowledge, warmth, and success. The heat of the flame brings sympathetic comfort. But it also burns, exorcizing you from fiery ill-thinkers and do-ers with their own demons. She and her faithful infernal black dog torment people trying to sidetrack, upset, or use you. Someone may encourage you to go off route since your company suits their journey, but this may get you lost or delay you reaching your destination.

Your love life looks very promising. Elen's torch means someone holds a flaming torch of love, passion, and desire for you. A person from your past gravely regrets not being with you today. If you are alone without a lover, you are about to cross paths with someone who will reveal their love to you, warming your heart while offering enduring love.

In the game of life and its battles you will have outstanding victory. If you're a sports competitor, you will win prizes and fame in games. Elen athletically

assists your victory in sports events. Her torch is the Olympic torch, symbol of the Olympic Games, and the Flame of Hope, associated with the Special Olympics—an icon of hope and light, when there seem to be no rays of light and hope at all. You appear to be on a winning streak when traveling your chosen road. You will overcome any obstacles and successfully reach your destination because you follow the right path, intuitively knowing what you want and heading for it without distractions or a flickering doubt. On principle, you keep the light within you lit.

ELEN'S MESSAGE The witching hour at midnight is Elen's greatest hour. She'll see you through moments of despair since daylight always follows night. Look before you leap. Consider your motives when making decisions. Use willpower so your spirit rules the body. Keep going to the end of the road and enjoy the journey.

ELEN'S SPELL TO REMOVE A PROBLEM Write your problem to Elen on a piece of white paper. At midnight, burn the piece of paper in a candle flame and say: *"May Elen's light be above me and beneath me, to the left and to the right of me, behind me and in front of me, and may Elen's light guide me every day and night."* Snuff the candle out before bedtime or leave it to burn down safely. Or, bury the piece of paper at a three-way crossroads. Leave a food offering such as bird seed or a piece of bread on top of the earth covering the buried paper.

Coventina

GODDESS OF HAPPINESS

KEYWORDS: Joy • Regeneration • Exuberance

COUNTRY OF ORIGIN: Scotland

Coventina is the goddess of wells and water. You have tapped into a spring of happiness that won't run dry. Your right thinking has a healing effect and divinely turned thought is a powerful positive force. Your happiness depends on your temperament, not problems and circumstances. Like Coventina's well, happiness begins from within and receives from without. You are fulfilling your own happiness because what you are is what you want to be.

Happy surprises are due. You may be going on a sunny vacation. You will certainly get what you want and like what you get. This will come your way through someone you know—family, a co-worker, or a friend. Your life is looking less difficult now you're choosing not to let minor irritations upset you. Your actions make you contented because what you think, do, and say is in harmony. Your endeavors to try to overcome a difficult mission will bring you exuberance, since this goddess suggests that you will succeed and enjoy watching each stage reach fruition.

You have peace of mind and self-respect, knowing in the depths of your soul that you are your own reliable best friend, similar to Coventina's dependable well water that can always be drawn from the depths to the surface. You always have

higher rather than lower thoughts, so doubt never worries you. Others will gravitate around you, escalating both your happiness and theirs.

A celebration is forecast and is an opportunity to be among empowering people, not drainers. Socially, your happiness is increasing and involves sports, hobbies, organizations, and your career. You'll be doing something you love and have hoped for, including loving and being loved, which makes you feel secure.

Happiness will emerge from a seemingly hopeless situation. Even when facing adversity, good things can spring from its source. When you replace negative thoughts with empowering ones, you'll manifest healthy, life-changing situations. You'll be with people who encourage you to be better, since the forces for you are stronger than those against you.

You want happiness more than anything, and your joy is spreading to those around you. People will remember that you made them feel happier, even if they forget your words. From today, happiness will brighten your life. You will sometimes have what you want when you want it, but when you don't, pray for people to help you. God always provides, as symbolized by Coventina's well that

never runs dry. Keep positive. When something doesn't work out, things can still turn out well in a different way. Keep going faithfully with an open mind, and in the fullness of time you'll see your path and then you will look back and understand. If there is something that must be done, do it and you'll feel more enthusiastic and confident. You will get the right job, home, and partner.

You'll spend time doing things you like and move away from recent difficulties. You have dates in your diary and sunshine to look forward to. Your happiness is coming from unexpected positive events, bringing lasting peace in a satisfying way. You will be appreciated and rewarded due to your purposeful actions.

COVENTINA'S MESSAGE You will count your blessings, not troubles. Your unwavering willpower to feel happy now, and not postpone this until cheerful events arrive, is the spring of knowledge Coventina represents; knowing everything you do is the best you can do gives you peace. Happiness is a state of mind, and life can go well whatever your circumstances. Your self-reliance reinforces your self-respect.

COVENTINA'S PREDICTION SPELL Light a candle, then stare at the flame and tell it to rise. It will. Ask a question that can be answered with a "yes" or "no." If the flame flickers to the right, the answer is "yes." If it flickers to the left, the answer is "no." Tell the flame what you want in your life or explain how you would like a particular problem to be resolved in your favor.

Brigit

GODDESS OF HOME COMFORTS

KEYWORDS: Security • Well-being • Nourishment

COUNTRY OF ORIGIN: Ireland

Brigit symbolizes pure, bright eternal light in the form of a flame that rises from Earth to Heaven, embodying the elements of earth and fire. Brigit is the virgin goddess of the hearth, where love, warmth, and protection abound. In exchange for personal and family blessings, a cross woven from rushes is made to honor Brigit on Imbolg (February 1), a time when new spring bulbs prove winter is ending and brighter days are coming. Your life is serene with easier times ahead.

Although revered as a virgin, Brigit is called "mother," since the hearth is feminine compared to the masculine flames. Brigit represents chastity and virtue. She rejected marriage, preferring fidelity and purity—so is a sign you may reject an unworthy lover. An old flame may return to rekindle a relationship or someone you haven't heard from for a while may appear with a gift.

Brigit also protects maternity and seeds sown in fields, and presides over nourishment from nature's harvest. Through pure food and lifestyle, light is nourished in the body, so you live in harmony physically and spiritually. Keeping the sacred fire alight within you is to keep contact with the power of the universe. A person's body is their spirit's hearth. Honoring the fire's flames is to activate personal powerful qualities, fueled by ingenuity and momentum.

Things you want in your present home will come. You will find a new home if you're trying to move. If you don't give a key to your lover, you're not giving the key to your heart. You are resourceful, organized, and sparkling with wit, like the sparks flying from Brigit's fire. Sparks of love are shooting in your direction, igniting a happy relationship. There will be peace of mind now and in your future.

Something spectacular is going to happen that will light up your life, pleasing you and those you know. You'll succeed in matters of the heart, home, and family, and enjoy home comforts in relaxing, good company. Warm thoughts around you bring a party invitation to another's home or a venue. You're also a great source of hospitality and comfort to someone else.

Don't allow someone to shoot down in flames an idea you feel strongly about.

BRIGIT'S MESSAGE Your ignited creativity brings success to you, your home, and family. Don't allow someone to shoot down in flames an idea you feel strongly about. Cling to the flame of hope, faith, and optimism in your heart. The flame symbolizes transcendence and spreads light on you and your endeavors. Since you've connected to the light, you are protected by it. Flames need fuel if they are not to burn out. Faith is your fuel.

PYROMANCY Pyromancy is fire divination. Here are Brigit's fireside predictions (which are also seen in bonfires and barbecues):

- Sparks reveal you'll receive an invitation.
- Bluish embers are believed to be good spirits telling you things are getting better. They also signify ill health improving.
- A heart shape represents new love if you are single or fidelity from your lover if you're in a relationship.
- Coin shapes mean money is coming to you soon.
- Embers that look like stairs or a ladder mean a wish will come true. If the embers are bright, the wish will be granted soon; if dark, not quite yet.
- A fire burning on one side is a sign of a quarrel with someone or a separation.

- A fire still alight in the morning signifies you will have company.
- A roaring fire means you will hear words of disapproval, while a blazing fire means someone is burning with passion for you.
- Peeling soot foretells communication from an absent friend or acquaintance.
- Soot drawn into the fire means someone will come to stay.
- Soot dropping onto the hearth means someone you'd like to see will not arrive.
- For a wish to be granted, write it on a piece of paper and throw it into a blazing fire to burn. If the piece of paper flies up the chimney, your wish will come true spectacularly and quickly.

Branwen

GODDESS OF EMOTIONS

KEYWORDS: Accord • Kindness • Gentleness

COUNTRY OF ORIGIN: Ireland

Branwen, queen of the night, shows that darkness cannot hide the radiance of your life since you are able to reflect light. Hold on to your inner light, and trust that there is a fundamental justice in the universe. Keep your faith and remain undaunted in an uphill struggle. As the full moon waxes and wanes, so do your emotions and circumstances. However dark a situation, light will reappear.

The clouds around Branwen mean a good transformation is taking place, as clouds are always changing. You'll cultivate the positive as an antidote to what you want to eliminate and your problems will fade like evaporating clouds. Stare at a cloud and tell it a problem. Ask the cloud to move right or left. Look away for a few minutes, then look again and the cloud will have evaporated, like your problem, revealing blue skies of happiness for you. You'll receive good news that sets you on a path to success and good luck will not desert you. A wish will be granted since Branwen represents wish fulfillment, good luck, and companionship.

Fertility and sexuality in a relationship, work, or a home project are predicted by Branwen's starling, as starlings quickly multiply. Do not be afraid to take a leap of faith, like a starling taking flight. Experience has taught you that possession is better than expectation.

Like a waxing moon, move forward and be receptive to a new relationship, rather than yearn for a previous lover to change. Branwen received protection from a starling when fleeing her tyrannical husband. She sent it across the Irish Sea to her brother in Wales, who traveled to rescue her. Likewise, you are being rescued from difficulties. You will socialize with new people who share your interests and spread your wings socially. You may travel to where there is a river or lake, or overseas. Just as the full moon's magnetism creates a tidal wave, so it has the power to change your fortune when you go with the flow. When the moon is full, your psychic powers are highly illuminated. Be reassured that sadness, poverty, and ill health can turn to happiness, riches, and good health, as reliably as a full moon never fails to wane to a new moon.

You will break free and attain higher realms since your soul is elevated by thoughts, like a flying bird. If a bird visits you, it may carry the soul of a loved one, able to answer a question you ask. The answer is "yes" if the bird flies to the right and "no" if it flies to the left. Someone is going to trust you with extraordinary knowledge. If you're waiting for another person's decision, you will soon have it. The next full moon or first day of next month will be significantly good for you.

BRANWEN'S MESSAGE You will deal with and remove a problem. Branwen indicates you'll enjoy brightness, gentleness, and harmony. A family celebration or reunion will happen. The moon, which carries emotions, reveals disputes with loved ones will be settled. You know it's in your best interest to forgive to avoid carrying the burden of discontent. Your relatives will advise how to handle a predicament as well as offer physical and financial help. Happiness, good luck, and exuberance are yours, imbuing you with the peace of mind to feel loving, sympathetic, kind, calm, and confident, not fearful or angry.

BRANWEN'S GOOD LUCK SPELL Cast this spell at any time, not just when the moon is full. Cut a circle from a piece of white paper to represent a full moon. Write your wishes on the paper moon, then place it beneath a white tealight or candle. Light the candle and say your wishes aloud. Around your waist, imagine a circle of gold light for protection and a circle of blue light for healing. When the candle is extinguished, fold the paper moon in half and then in half again. Keep the piece of paper in your purse until you receive your wish fulfillment, then bury or burn the piece of paper.

BRANWEN'S MAKE A WISH SPELL When there is a full moon you might like to draw down the moon. Look at the moon's reflection in a pond, lake, or the sea, and say your wishes out loud to the reflection. Calmness will imbue you.

Aimend

GODDESS OF GOOD HEALTH

KEYWORDS: Intuition • Vitality • Nutrition

COUNTRY OF ORIGIN: Ireland

Aimend is the goddess of fertility, health, healing, regeneration, and rebirth, and will bring positivity to all your endeavors. Her name means "sunburn," so rest assured you will be enjoying brighter days, living life to the full. Heavenly blessings will bring breakthroughs, introductions to life-changing people, and a much brighter future. Your intuition is more alert as heavenly maternal forces are nurturing you with gentleness, awakening your femininity to see from a higher perspective. Aimend symbolizes your higher self and own parent advising you. Listen to her as your mother wants to protect, nurture, and see you shine brightly.

Your life is blessed by divine intervention. It's being changed for the better, as if by a fairy godmother. If your mother has passed on, she's speaking to you from the spirit world. You'll meet her in a dream if you ask for this before you go to sleep. You'll visit the coast and book a sunny vacation abroad. You'll experience revival in a project or aim by meeting someone new. News will arrive from a long-lost friend, bringing renewal to your relationship. Difficult decisions will be more straightforward with your broader, more optimistic outlook and energy.

You're entering a positive phase by being welcomed into an inner circle of influential people.

They'll help you cultivate your dreams and find a niche in life that brings money and contentment. Listen to your higher self and ignore anyone who says your dreams won't come true. Their voices are the enemy trying to create disorder and derail you. You'll have power to see more clearly when you watch what is happening. Listen and connect to new people sent by heavenly intervention. You have just met them or will within a matter of weeks. Spring is also significant for meeting these people who will change your life for the better.

Like a flame, rise above your situation. Look at a predicament from a higher perspective while clinging to your foundation. Put yourself first and question the motives behind another person's plans for you. Don't let takers use your precious time. False friends shadow you while your life has something for them, but vanish when difficulties arise. Go forward and shake off what is now behind you.

You'll be proactive in bringing about what you want. If you believe you can succeed, you will. Every dawn brings renewed strength and sunshine makes you feel brighter. Crops cannot grow without its heat and light. Aimend presides over nutrition, grains, pulses, vegetables, fruits, and

herbs for healing. Eating natural foods puts you in harmony with Mother Nature, keeping body and spirit alive.

AIMEND'S MESSAGE Don't go against Mother Nature or your personal intuition. Don't ever give up and you won't be defeated—if you weather a storm, the sun will always reappear. Consider the seeds you sow and how they bear fruit. Focus on what will make life better and resist being diverted. Works of Mother Nature are doing what she has directed you to do. She speaks to your heart and soul, and you feel comfortable in your body.

AIMEND'S SPELLS FOR GOOD HEALTH

- Take some flowering bulbs and hair from your brush. Place a few stones in a pot and put the hair on top. Sprinkle with potting compost and arrange the bulbs in a circle, saying: *"My health is improving, I have good health, I will always have good health. As the bulbs grow, so will my health."* Fill the pot with potting compost. As the bulbs root and grow, so will your good health.

- Place some dried lavender, three bay leaves, and three dried lima (butter) beans in the center of a handkerchief. Gather together the corners of the handkerchief and tie the ingredients into a ball with red ribbon or string. Place the handkerchief beside a red candle and light the candle. Look at the flame and say: *"I take the light of this flame into my mind, body, and soul. Thank you for continuing my good health."* Let the candle burn for a while before snuffing it out. Keep the pouch in a bedroom drawer or carry it around with you.

Scathach

GODDESS OF THE MIND

KEYWORDS: Insight • Ingenuity • Versatility

COUNTRY OF ORIGIN: Scotland

Scathach reigns over the Spring Equinox (March 21). Her castle, Dun Sgathaich, stands on the Isle of Skye, in Scotland. Presiding over the disciplined use of war to protect from invasion, Scathach is a constant friend and advisor in military concerns. She advocates speaking up for yourself or redefining your boundaries to defend yourself from invasive people or situations. Your destiny is too important for you to be sidetracked. If you have something to do that you dislike doing, tell yourself you love doing it! You may be at war with yourself. Delusions can trick the mind. Scathach, known as the Shadow and Warrior Maid, teaches combating your fears and not to be afraid of yourself.

Scathach's spear indicates you'll hit any target you aim for. Scathach stands in encouragement and support of your aspirations. By successfully hitting your aim, unsupportive people will feel intimidated for not having believed in you.

Life is full of challenges, but your mind can overcome anything. Fate brings choices that open doors to good and bad fortune, wealth and poverty, ease and difficulties. You'll learn how to control fate, and whatever problem you have will be resolved in your favor. Even misfortune can be followed by good fortune. You'll overcome whatever you are struggling with, as Scathach personifies the wisdom needed to win battles. Scottish warriors taught martial arts by Scathach won their wars. Whether you're in dispute with a person or organization, victory will come, as you are protected from enemies and helped by people on your side.

Your vital energy is being awakened and elevated to deal with a problem or dispute. As in the martial arts taught by Scathach, your mindset defines your accomplishment. Winning is everything to do with the way you think about it and see it. A sudden idea spurs you on to feel stronger in mind, body, and spirit in order to persevere at this difficult time. The key to success is not to give up. You'll open the door to victory if you do not allow a problem to overwhelm or defeat you. When you keep on top of challenges, you'll eventually be victorious.

Great pearls of wisdom can be discovered if you count your blessings. You can create a harmonious whole by weighing the pros and cons to achieve equilibrium. Courageously discard outlived or destructive tendencies and replace them with better and wiser ones. Decide to be happy and expect something good to come your way. Do not be at war with yourself. Tell yourself that you like you, and make yourself likeable to you.

Spring brings new beginnings, the hatching of new plans, and seeds to sow, till, and tend. Life is balancing in your favor and getting brighter with each new day. You have a brilliant long spell of good fortune to look forward to.

SCATHACH'S MESSAGE Your battles will be won due to your fiery enthusiasm and courage, and the strength of your decision not to be defeated. Your efforts are not in vain even if you lose, since you stay motivated and persevere until the problem is resolved. It can be a struggle to stay on the side of good, but keep battling on, as it would be upsetting to lose. You know how to protect yourself from harm. Don't be foolish. Be wise. The universe is encouraging you not to go against the laws of nature, or you'll have to deal with the consequences later.

SCATHACH'S SPELL TO ACHIEVE YOUR AIM On the Spring Equinox, pierce a candle with a pin while saying your aim aloud. Light the candle. Allow the candle to burn through the pin, then snuff it out. Bury the candle stub and pin.

SCATHACH'S SPELL TO WIN A BATTLE Say to Scathach: *"I block and resist all negativity coming to me from [name the person or organization] and send it to God and the universe to deal with."* Higher forces will deal with the problem for you, bit by bit, and you won't absorb the negativity. Or, when the weather is stormy, imagine capturing light from the lightning into yourself. As the thunder sounds, say the problem out loud and command the thunder to take it away.

Cliodna

GODDESS OF BEAUTY

KEYWORDS: Serenity • Triumph • Sixth sense

COUNTRY OF ORIGIN: Ireland

Cliodna is symbolic of the Celtic afterlife and water magic. You're in for a beautiful time beyond your expectations and heavenly situations are possible. Cliodna's beauty is radiating from within and you're getting better at loving yourself and staying positive. Your self-belief is making you stronger and your sense of humor is attracting other people. Your confidence is growing and shows in your appearance. Without having to seek it out, you're finding beauty and happiness within. No matter what the situation, there can be a beautiful outcome even after disaster. With misfortune encouraging you to put a plan into action, you are assured of more success and a higher state of spiritual development and esoteric knowledge. Your faith and hope assist higher forces who intertwine circumstances into your life to put you in sync with the cosmos and people.

You'll always be safe when you believe in yourself and have faith in the higher forces guiding you. Anyone trying to deflect you from your goal will be proved wrong. Cliodna drowned in the sea when she left the "Land of Promise" to be with her human lover Ciabhan. The message of this story is to let your head rule your heart. Think carefully before you follow a partner's plans or another's schemes. Cliodna's spirit lives in the rocks where she

floundered, meaning there is a danger of hitting rock bottom if your decisions are not self-governed and your motivation as steady as a rock. Cliodna's three colorful birds represent air, faith, and contemplation. They eat apples from a heavenly tree, meaning you should value what you have and not throw it away for someone worthless.

Cliodna's tree connects Heaven to the Earth since the branches are in the sky and the roots in the earth. This means you'd be foolish not to depend on a reciprocal union. If money is not plentiful, this is a sign you're working to the tree top and will climb out of debt. You'll meet someone who already regards you as important. You'll leave people who could spoil a careful plan. Expect emotional good fortune from people in high places who will help you attain your dreams.

You are beautiful because of your beautiful soul. A kind personality is lovelier than attractive features. You will see the beauty of nature reinforce your body and soul. You will appreciate the spirit contact you receive. Cliodna may inspire spirit messages, which will take the form of a flow of ideas when you're handling water at home or near water in nature.

CLIODNA'S MESSAGE Avoid damaging thoughts and be ruled by positive ones. Re-examine your priorities. The day will be less overwhelming if you ask the powers above to help you. To maintain harmony, give compliments and encouragement. Value people the way they are.

BIRD OMENS Birds carry messages to and from God and are divinatory signs. Ask a question for an answer to a situation:

- Birds flying right to left means "yes" and from left to right means "no."
- A bird flying toward you means good news is coming your way, while a bird ascending almost vertically reveals immediate triumph for you.
- A bird flying against the wind warns of rough times since someone is being deceitful, failing to honor their word, or respect what you've asked them to do.

FINDING A FEATHER Finding a feather is believed to be a heaven-sent message.

- **WHITE** is a sign you will have peace of mind. Black means the imminent end of a bad situation. **YELLOW** signifies you'll be congratulated. **PINK** means romance will blossom. **BLUE** is a sign of emotional or physical healing. Your circumstances are becoming less problematic. **RED** means you'll feel renewed vitality. **GREEN** conveys financial increase and sexual fertility. **TURQUOISE** means freedom from pressure, relaxation, and enjoyment. **BROWN** reveals mental and physical harmony for you.
- A **BLACK-AND-WHITE** feather (or separate feathers of those colors) reveals dangers have been overcome. A **BROWN-AND-WHITE** feather (or one or more feathers of each of those colors) predicts improvements in wealth and desires being fulfilled.

Cred

GODDESS OF CLAIRVOYANCE

KEYWORDS: Foresight • Connection • Help

COUNTRY OF ORIGIN: Ireland

Goddess of clairvoyance and spirit contact, Cred vowed to marry only a clairvoyant man who could describe her home in poetry without seeing it. If you are searching for a love-match, this goddess will assist you in meeting your twin flame who shares the same vision of a future with you.

Your psychic powers are reawakening within you and becoming stronger. Your destiny will be revealed to you in visionary dreams. A person who you already know or someone you are about to meet is linking you to a new pathway to success in love or work. You will feel comfortable with this new connection. Accepting an offer made will feel like the right thing to do. The right frequency is that place which tells you morally, physically, and spiritually that you feel comfortable. What sits right with your conscience is the right frequency. This will be easy for you to find simply by being yourself, and weighing up choices, invitations, and opportunities.

When you follow what your own intuition is trying to tell you, you will not make mistakes. You will find your personal frequency of divine intervention linking to you and encouraging you to believe in yourself and not lose sight of your ambitions—instead, persevere with what you instinctively know is right.

The right partner is near you now or is entering your life over the next few months. That person is someone who understands your clairvoyance and is sympathetic to you. He or she values you, is supportive, and not fearful of your ability to see through other people.

A phone call, communication, personal meeting, or get-together will lead to the end result you've been keeping on course to achieve without giving in to distractions. The spirit world is sending people your way to help you make the right connections in life. You'll recognize them as being heaven-sent. If you're unsure whether what you think is right, ask for confirmation from the spirit world. A sign or message will be given to you visually or audibly.

You are conquering yourself and your immediate environment, which puts you in a higher position and level of existence than you have been of late. You are attaining a high stage of development because your spirit is ruling your body and your willpower is ruling your mind. You can expect an easy victory and crowning achievement because your higher principles are ruling base instincts.

A powerful person you know is going to open a door for you by communicating with someone in a

high position. You'll soar to great heights. Far-flung travel is also presenting itself to you.

You're on the threshold of a charming life situation. Many people will be rallying around to help you get to where you want to be. You will differentiate between genuine and ungenuine people and situations. You will find that you belong in well-respected company. You win a crown of success by conquering yourself.

CRED'S MESSAGE Avoid sending psychic bullets by speaking ill of someone who has wronged or hurt you. Your optimistic faith brings you success if you put the situation in the hands of the universe. Put a cloak of light around you when you enter another person's home because you bring psychic thoughts into their home. You will dream premonitions that will come true. You have a God-given gift of psychic powers. You thank God for your gift by using it.

CRED'S SPELL FOR CLAIRVOYANCE Light a candle of any color. Turn off all electric lights. Stare at the flame for three minutes. You will see a ring of light encircling the flame composed of all the colors of the rainbow. Close your eyes and keep them closed for three or more minutes. In your mind's eye (your clairvoyant eye or third eye), you'll see the flame and the ring around it and then visions. The visions are psychic. The people you see may be your spirit guides. If you wish, look at the flame again for a few minutes, then close your eyes for more clairvoyant visions.

Modron

GODDESS OF MOTHERHOOD

KEYWORDS: Fertility • Nurturing • Affection

COUNTRY OF ORIGIN: Wales

Modron is a healer and the goddess of women, children, fertility, and boys until they are men. Since you love something or someone, you'll be enthusiastic and creative—what you are trying to give birth to will develop, as you will nurture every stage of the journey with affection. You will speak to yourself in a kind, maternal way that brings peace of mind. You will also meet someone who sparks spontaneity in you. As if with heavenly maternal gentleness, you will be rewarded for your trust, faith, and intuition, so your wants and needs are met and your anxiety ended. Modron, a "Divine Mother," can intercede when asked to.

If your mother has passed on, she'll make her protective presence felt as the link of love continues after death. Being spirit she can move you to the right place, at the right time, with the right people. Her words of eternal wisdom will grow in you and you'll recognize some of them as predictions.

You will be around respectful people and in places you can enjoy Mother Nature. You'll probably change your diet so you are nurtured by Mother Nature's life-giving grains, pulses, vegetables, fruits, and nuts. You're in harmony with nature and in sync with the universe when you eat this health-giving harvest. People need Mother

Earth, but she can probably survive much better without us.

If you believe you can give birth to aspirations, you'll get fruitful results, as symbolized by Modron's fruit, bread, and babies. You may be a loving mother or yet to become one. You will reap the fruits of your labors by planting the seeds today. People who appreciate your care are strengthening you. Someone in a better position will inspire you to follow their ethics, hard work, and confidence. Your receptivity to others means you'll always attract people's help. Have faith, keep focused, and finish what needs to be done, as you'll find Mother Nature will reward you. She cannot be outwitted and always wins, so go along with her.

What is about to transpire will make you feel blessed by a fairy godmother. Your feminine intuition is strong. You can know things about a person by looking at their face; detect truth from lies when you listen to someone; and sense when something feels good or bad. Evil's most powerful weapon is deception disguised as something that looks attractive.

You will make sacrifices, just as a mother does for her child and create something enduring. You'll communicate with a person you trust. Others will

Modron is a healer and the goddess of women, children, fertility, and boys until they are men.

make sacrifices for you, as you deserve love from them and yourself. True love is so powerful: it conquers all. You're beloved when you give love and will reap what you sow.

MODRON'S MESSAGE Be nurtured by Mother Nature. Love your mother and listen to her—she has known you longer than anyone. Communicate with your mother and be guided by her in a situation in your life. Reconnect with nature and your mother when you need guidance. You'll receive news of a pregnancy. Bread represents the life force; a wheat grain symbolizes birth and death in human life. Cut corn signifies death that is reborn, just as wheat grain grows into food. Life and death, rebirth and resurrection are holy. Like Modron's fruit, human life has succulent seasons that fade with time. Something innocent in you is attracting new beginnings and purity in love relationships, as symbolized by Modron's babies.

MODRON'S SPELL FOR THE BIRTH OF AN AMBITION Take a long, red candle and a long, gold candle to represent wealth. From the tip to midway and the base to midway, smear peppermint oil (communication and protection) on the red candle and rose oil (love) on the gold one. Place the candles side by side in holders before a mirror and light them. Write an ambition on gold card and place it face up in front of the candles. Look at the flames and say: *"It is my ambition to be a [name this]. Open the doors for my success. I am a success and will be a success doing or being a [name this]."* Let the candles burn down, then snuff them out. Put the card in a purse and work at your ambition. Your spell will come true in time.

Anu

GODDESS OF PROSPERITY

KEYWORDS: Success • Celebration • Money

COUNTRY OF ORIGIN: Ireland

A symbol of good fortune and beauty, Anu is a comforter and healer, a light even in a person's darkest hour. She advocates financial and spiritual wealth; light over darkness, or good over evil; knowledge above ignorance; and hope above despair. Anu is welcoming you to ask her for what you want in life. She will give you powerful magical and practical help to light up your life. Beautiful blessings and good fortune from on high will suddenly make your situation transparent. You will experience a rejuvenation of feminine wisdom and rapidly make money or receive physical gifts and presents. If you apply for a job, you will get it. Or you will be in a position to buy something you have been aiming to. Just as Anu's waterfall stands as a connection between Heaven and Earth, all good things are now flowing your way. There is a dissolving of obstacles and a washing away of worries, bringing pure, heaven-sent freshness to current projects and renewed energy for new beginnings.

You will be embracing financial wealth and supreme heavenly power to completely fulfill your four goals in life, which are: to live a moral, principled existence, to pursue wealth and a way of life that earns a living, to pursue faithful love and emotional happiness, and to pursue self-knowledge and freedom. The regal swans of Anu symbolize that you possess a gift for prophecy and faithful love. Your revelations will deliver you fine expectations, promises, and serene knowing as you progress toward your aim in life. If beneath the surface you are furiously struggling to keep afloat, you will maintain your balance and achieve the satisfaction of your desire with noble purity. You will not sink, but will have victory over your struggles with dignity. Like a dying swan that beautifully sings its last breaths, you'll be singing with joy that a bad or difficult situation is ending. Liberating elements are rearranging a happier lifestyle for you.

The daisy that opens at sunrise and closes at sunset represents compassion and the emergence of light—in the same way, you are coming out of a less than happy time into the sunshine of brighter days, in which you will always enjoy periods of plenty. You're about to put in a first appearance, or a newcomer or welcomed new venture will appear in your life through your actions. Regardless of your position, prosperity and good can blossom and bloom. You will increase your possessions, friends, and power, making you vulnerable to the needs of others who hold you in high esteem for your strong, maternal, feminine instincts.

Red, the color of Anu's hair, is the color of magic, which is the most powerful of all weapons. Forces behind the scenes are weaving enchantment into your projects and plans. You'll feel lighter, as if elevated, because someone is being sent to assist you over a hurdle. Their intelligence and expertise will free you and resolve a problem that you will steadily win.

ANU'S MESSAGE Anu's divine magical and powerful, practical strength represents you when you achieve your aims in love and work. She advocates the importance of balancing economic and academic activity with spiritual learning, so the two work together to bring complete fulfillment. You are destined to overcome obstacles and rise high in life.

ANU'S SPELL FOR FINANCIAL PROSPERITY If you've hit hard financial times or simply wish to invite good fortune, happiness, and riches into your home. Take four bay leaves and write your wishes for money or anything else on them. Put a silver-colored coin on top of each bay leaf. Light a white candle. Look at the flame and then the image of the goddess while saying: *"Anu, please bring abundance to me."* Let the candle burn to a stub and bury it at a time that suits you. In the morning, place the coins indoors above or beside your front door or under the inside doormat. Keep the bay leaves in a small envelope in your purse for 28 days. Then bury them in your garden or in nature.

Ban-Chuideachaidh Moire

GODDESS OF CHILDBIRTH AND YOUTH

KEYWORDS: Devotion • Practicality • Forgiveness

COUNTRY OF ORIGIN: Ireland

A new beginning is being offered to you, symbolized by Ban-Chuideachaidh Moire, the goddess of childbirth and cupbearer to gods and goddesses. She is said to have helped Mary give birth to Jesus. Ban-Chuideachaidh Moire is symbolized by a fountain of eternal youth, which means when you tap into the fountain of your God-given creativity, you become innocently youthful and achieve what you were born to. She advocates a pure lifestyle in youth, so bad habits don't create problems that will need to be dealt with when wisdom comes. We learn in youth; we understand in age. Youth presents opportunities not to take the wrong path since it is protected and sheltered by parents and guardians.

Ban-Chuideachaidh Moire's gift of eternal youth is to be creative. She was devoted to domestic occupations. Her spring cleaning is spiritual as well as making physical improvements to the home or preparations for an important visitor, new family member, or pet. Loving your life keeps you youthful. You will be rejuvenated by finding happiness in what you do, as it keeps the fountain of youth flowing. You'll find the balance by making each day both practical and pleasant. Understanding the value of time means you will put it to the best possible use.

Like youth, time passes. In your lifetime, each day is a miniscule life. In youth, the days are brief and full and the years long, but in old age the years are brief, and may be empty, and the days long.

Ban-Chuideachaidh Moire's sacred goblet offers you true love, friendship, enjoyment, and satisfaction. You may receive a commitment from a loved one, or hear someone declare their love. If footloose, you're about to encounter a new love that will grow from youthfulness to maturity. This romance can easily lead to engagement, a marriage made in heaven, or living together. You will have a pleasurable social life. You may receive an award for your achievements, hear of a house move, or receive sympathy and blessings from someone very fond of you. You can accomplish youthful dreams with fresh vitality and grasp opportunities.

The ivy crown Ban-Chuideachaidh Moire wears represents inspired thoughts. No storm can tear ivy from a tree, which means life's battles cannot wrench you from the purity you were born with. Ivy's evergreen leaves are an allegory for the eternal life of your soul, which should cling, like ivy, to the force that created it. This goddess is connected to childbirth, so projects you begin now, nurture, and protect will mature. You will be supported and

taught what you need to know, especially when you seek advice. You're in for a time of vivacity and fun with fewer worries and considerations than of late.

BAN-CHUIDEACHAIDH MOIRE'S MESSAGE

Personality, willpower, imagination, and strong emotions continue from childhood; cultivate them well, as they bring promise and hope to your future. There are many new things in the world to attract you. Form good habits in youth to pave the way for a less problematic future. Value each day as a miniature life: morning is birth and youth, afternoon is maturity, and night, death. Make the right choices in youth and reap the rewards. Make the right choices each morning and what follows will turn out well.

IVY "YES" OR "NO" ANSWER TO A QUESTION

To divine a "yes" or "no" answer to a question, place an ivy leaf in a dish of water for six days. If the leaf has no blemishes on the sixth day, the answer is "yes." The answer to your question is "no" if the leaf has blemishes.

IVY NEW YEAR'S EVE DIVINATION On New

Year's Eve, leave an ivy leaf in a dish of water until Twelfth Night (January 5). If by that time no blemishes have appeared on the leaf, it is a sign you'll have a very happy New Year. If dark spots have appeared on the leaf, it's an omen that the New Year will not be without difficulties.

Rosmerta

GODDESS OF COMMUNICATION

KEYWORDS: Harmony • Good news • Providence

COUNTRY OF ORIGIN: Ireland

Rosmerta is the bearer of good news and associated with a rainbow. This conveys the potential there is for good things to happen for you. Beginning today, little miracles, coincidences, and divine intervention fulfilling your desires will come to your attention. Life is becoming more colorful and varied, and you sincerely appreciate the small things you may have taken for granted in the past.

People near and far will be connecting with you and grateful people will thank you by sending a gift. People or a person from your past will appear. A person in a position of authority, who you're already close to, will establish a heaven-sent business contact, leading you to where you're meant to be. The transition will bring huge success. Like the fruits in Rosmerta's basket, something that may have taken a long time and a lot of patience to develop will lead to fruitfulness.

The light of Rosmerta's rainbow is a sign that heavenly light is protecting you. Heart-felt requests for help have been heard and what you need will be delivered. Your requests will be granted since Rosmerta is a carer and provider. Ask and you will receive a God-send that brings commercial success, emotional fulfillment, and better mental and physical stamina and health. Through divine benevolence,

good news or money, or both, will arrive. The seven colors of the rainbow confirm the promise there is for colorful, happy things to come your way. Since Rosmerta can take on human form, the spirit world will work through people you meet to help you make the right connections. Some will intuit the help you need, while others want you not to be too proud to ask. The winds of change are transforming your life for the better, symbolized by Rosmerta. She travels like the wind while her helpers slide down the rainbow to offer heavenly assistance.

You're not chasing rainbows but working hard toward your dreams. You feel as free as the wind and have the energy to complete a project. Like Rosmerta's fruit basket, your plans will be fruitful. Good news will prove you can expect a wealthy future, with financial stability and security being denoted by Rosmerta's purse.

You are elevated and connected to the heavenly realms, making you feel over the rainbow with happiness. You'll also experience a spiritual evolution, ensuring you value yourself more, appreciate your uniqueness, and discover a gift within. This will open up a new spectrum of spiritual contact and bring human friends, family, and commercial contacts your way.

Rosmerta's caduceus (or staff) means a cure from illness and convalescence, so expect to have improved health and find the people around you easier to get on with. Someone is now seeing things from your point of view, so you'll get what you want. They listen since what you say to them is worth hearing, just as you patiently listen to others. You have the pure energy of self-control, resulting in good mental, spiritual, and physical health and well-being.

ROSMERTA'S MESSAGE Rosmerta's rainbow means peace. Heaven hears your call and responds by blessing your heart-felt yearnings. Hold on to your hopes and dreams and keep believing that miracles can happen. Expect good news within days or a few weeks regarding work, money, love, or health. The life force of Rosmerta's rainbow reinforces your belief in spiritual protection. It is a reminder to recognize and know that there is more to life than the physical world. Your guardian angels, spirit guides, and human people will confirm everything is getting better for you. Uncertainty and fear are replaced by serenity and peace.

RAINBOW SUPERSTITIONS

- Make a wish when you see a rainbow and it will come true.
- It is said to be unlucky to point at a rainbow. Dreaming of a rainbow is a sign of imminent happiness.
- If you see a rainbow at a funeral, be assured it is a message from the deceased that they're at rest and want you to enjoy life rather than mourn for them.

Adsullata

GODDESS OF PRAYERS

KEYWORDS: Fulfillment • Spirituality • Inner peace

COUNTRY OF ORIGIN: Wales

Miracles are about to happen. Expect a big change to turn your life around. What occurs is the beginning of a new and long-lasting era. It may be meeting your marriage partner, moving home, starting a family, or a new job. None of your prayers are unheard or not answered. Adsullata, a messenger goddess of prayers, hears your call and carries your prayers and the longings of your soul to God. What you ask for will be delivered from heaven to you. Adsullata's kindness permeates you with her qualities. God works through you, so you answer other people's prayers through your positive words and practical deeds. You may not be aware you are answering other people's prayers and other people may not know they are answering yours.

You will know your prayers are being answered through physical manifestation, since signs will catch your attention. You may think of someone and they'll get in touch. Or someone important will come along, making things change without you expecting them to. The source of all possibilities flows your way when you pray because you put your life in sync. By having a conversation with God as you would talk to a friend, you can pray through your day, asking for guidance as it progresses. As time moves on into that day or week, you'll receive subtle spiritual signs

and prompts to confirm that you're linked to your prayers and answers. You may experience audible, physical, and other sixth-sense epiphanies. When you're about to make an important decision, a clairaudient voice in your mind may shout "yes" or "no." If you ask for forgiveness, it will be given, as the universe is a source of endless love to all on Earth, just like Adsullata's ever-flowing spring.

If you begin each day with a prayer, you've connected and will be protected. If you offer to be helpful to God each day, you'll naturally find your personal, purposeful niche in life. Don't think your prayers are unanswered if a physical result takes time to appear. Have faith, as time is needed for some connections to develop, or perhaps the universe has something better in store for you.

God is light and energy, and some people (like you) see God in nature. Prayer is a powerful connection with the greatest universal force. Prayer can be to your ancestors or those who've passed on. God speaks to a heart that feels comfortable within its body, so respect your body as a vehicle for your soul. If you pray for a problem to go away, it will fade if you deal with it rather than dwell on it. Good will win over evil when you stop negative thoughts captivating your mind. Pray for something

Good will win over evil when you stop negative thoughts captivating your mind

and you'll be shown how to get it. Works of God are carrying out what God has guided you to do. God will put thoughts into your mind if you listen carefully when you pray.

Prayer gives you peace and the power to change your circumstances, as shown by Adsullata's phial, a symbol of salvation. Her willow twig signifies an endless source of wisdom which is believed to heal ill-health and ward off evil. A prayer can't be answered if you do not pray for what you want. If a request is meant to be granted, it will not pass you by. You'll receive daily acts of kindness, while being more sympathetic to others than they deserve.

ADSULLATA'S MESSAGE Prayer is only good for you. Your spirit will grow stronger and you'll become a better person if you channel the power of the universe into every part of your life. Your sense of self-worth will increase. Ask for what you need, be watchful, and you'll notice your prayers being granted through people you know or those you meet. Prayer brings you peace of mind by putting you in the right place at the right time. Discovering your gift for inner peace, you'll find spirituality in any situation. Say every day: *"A miracle will happen today."* Your belief in a supernatural power manifests the miracle since you've connected to it.

ADSULLATA'S PRAYER SPELL Light a votive candle, then pray for what you want or say thanks for what you have. The energy will rise, even if you're not in the same room.

Latiaran

GODDESS OF MAGIC

KEYWORDS: Action • Pleasures • Otherworldly

COUNTRY OF ORIGIN: Ireland

An abundance of invitations and pleasurable meetings are coming your way, so seize these opportunities. What transpires will lead you to reaping harvests of gold and future happiness. In fact, you may feel as if Latiaran has cast her magic wand over your life. The harvest month of August is particularly fortuitous for getting what you want or going where you wish to go.

Now is the perfect time to sow the seeds for your future financial prosperity and emotional happiness. A new creative project you begin will bear fruit. You'll yield good results from your natural talents while enjoying being yourself. You'll derive pleasure and wealth from being inventive and exploring new interests. In relationships you are now thinking of settling. You may start a family, greet a new family member, or meet up with relatives or a loved one you rarely see.

Yet you must sow the seeds of hard work to reap a harvest. This is easier if you replace negative thoughts with positive ones. Your optimistic energy increases your yield and makes everything you do, better. Being among positive people encourages you to stay motivated. Something you need and have saved for, such as a home, car, or vacation, will give you pleasure. You may want to cut up your credit cards

and get out of debt by not wasting money on bank charges. Instead, you'll delight in the satisfaction and security of saving money. After all, Latiaran represents harvesting what you can to save for the future.

You have the mental strength to face any challenges even if you feel insecure about getting the result you want. Trust that spirit is leading you when you experience a fear of the unknown. Just take the first steps and see where they lead, as you'll grow in strength while surmounting your difficulties.

Latiaran had a magic wand to transform her enemies into wild animals. By being direct and straight with your enemies, like Latiaran's wand, you'll have your own enemies cornered. Like animals, they may scare you, but they won't win. The distress of an ordeal you have experienced is ending, resulting in your desired outcome. Keep heading for your destination, as you will eventually arrive.

Not only will you be enjoying the simple things in life that you can see, hear, smell, taste, and touch but other pleasures too. Your sixth sense is increasing, so you will push your confidence to feel at ease beyond your comfort zone.

A new direction beckons. This may be a satisfying sport or hobby, academic study, interior design, landscaping, arts and crafts, or learning about healthy eating, alternative medicine, or perfumery. Latiaran had a vast knowledge of herbal medicine and potions. Now is the time to follow your enthusiasm for something productive that you feel you'd like to do. You have much to look forward to and are assured of a brilliant time, especially between spring and late fall when all areas of your life will become as you wish.

LATIARAN'S MESSAGE You have an extraordinary ability to make things happen. You are a goddess of magic since you can transform any situation into something good for yourself and others. You possess the power to turn adversity into victory. Latiaran presides over Lughnasadh (July 31), the beginning of the harvest. Sow good seeds of ambition and heart-felt desires, and you'll reap beautiful results.

LATIARAN'S WISHES SPELL The full moon nearest the Fall Equinox (September 21) is the most potent time for this spell, but cast it at any time. Put some wheat grain in a dish beside a candle. Light the candle and tell the flame what you want to materialize in your life. For each desire, take a grain and place it in another dish. Let the candle burn until you're ready to snuff it out. Throw the grains for each wish into your backyard or an open space for the birds. Bury the candle stub.

HARVEST SUPERSTITIONS If you see corn being harvested or transported, make a wish. Keep a corn dolly at home to represent the spirit of the grain bringing fertility to your plans and ambitions.

Cerridwen

GODDESS OF TRUTH

KEYWORDS: Authenticity • Divine inspiration • Good faith

COUNTRY OF ORIGIN: Wales

Cerridwen presides over the Fall Equinox (September 21) when the leaves fall from the trees and the branches are laid bare. In the same way, truth will reflect who you are. You will find happiness by being tactfully truthful with people and less critical. Your positivity is strengthening your inward and outer beauty. By reflecting on your life you're turning what is negative into something positive, so a difficult situation will bring success. By keeping faith good doors will swing open for you, while your self-image becomes more confident. By keeping your mind fixed on past success, not failure, you will focus on taking the next step toward your chosen destination. You're cultivating an optimistic outlook to perform positive actions. You'll do everything better with decisive, optimistic reflections rather than negative, fearful thoughts.

On reflection, you have the strength to say "no" to what is spoiling your life. You're getting better at avoiding blaming other people, since you're more aware of how your behavior affects them. Being self-content means you'll go through situations more happily. Your self-contented attitude works wonders with people, while your appearance, friends, and home are now a reflection of you, as you're being true to yourself. Since your self-belief

is strengthened, you're not distracted from taking the next steps forward. Your truthfulness will expose other people's deception or lies. They may see the truth differently, but that doesn't change it. Good fortune will come since the bare facts of a situation will be revealed, as is symbolized by Cerridwen's nudity. How you react will bring out the best in you.

Cerridwen's light-reflecting mirror is a symbol of divinity and truth, and means that you have the heavenly help needed to attain happiness and protection from evil. There is more to what can be seen with the physical eyes, and your clairvoyance will reveal what is beyond the obvious. Good results will come when you open your will to the light or to God. If you believe you can achieve something wonderful, you will get fantastic results. Greater achievements are possible because you have the mindset, willpower, desire, and determination to attain your vision. Your output is an echo of what you enjoy performing.

In solitude, you can reflect without a mirror on what is working for you. You're closer to the truth than you think and can solve your own problems. The way you view yourself is more important than how you look at other people. Someone will love

Promise you'll be your own best friend.

you for telling the truth, while another will be upset with you, so speak carefully.

Magical potions in witches' cauldrons relate to the transformative power of food for optimum health. Cerridwen's cauldron shows that you can improve your life since it symbolizes the magical change of spiritual nourishment and the physical transformation of earthly sustenance. What you put in the pot is a recipe for success if the spiritual and physical ingredients are healthy for your mind, body, and soul.

CERRIDWEN'S MESSAGE Find your true self through inner enlightenment and bring about transformation. Become wiser by seeing the truth. If you're honest, you'll do what is right and you won't pretend to be something that you're not. You'll feel at peace with yourself and others.

CERRIDWEN'S SPELLS TO BEFRIEND YOURSELF
Position a dish of water so it reflects the moon. Look at the moon, then at the reflection, and make a wish. Leave the dish or throw it away once the moon is no longer reflected in the water. Alternatively, sit in front of a mirror and light a candle. Stare at the flame, close your eyes for three minutes, then look at your reflection. Promise you'll be your own best friend. Talk kindly to yourself, stating your plans aloud and forgiving yourself for mistakes.

CERRIDWEN'S "YES" OR "NO" DIVINATION Ask a "yes" or "no" question while dipping a mirror in some water. If your mirrored reflection is barely visible, then the answer is "no." If you can see your reflection fairly clearly, the answer is "yes."

Druantia

GODDESS OF SILENCE

KEYWORDS: Calm • Reserve • Compassion

COUNTRY OF ORIGIN: Scotland

Druantia is Queen of the Druids and goddess of silence. You are enjoying the beauty of silence, as it gives you the chance to think clearly. When your mind is quiet, especially in the silence before dawn, you can receive spirit messages. Listen and understand the answers to your questions. You'll be guided on how to plan that day and handle a current situation. You'll know you're close to spirit when you're silent, feel thoughts entering your mind, and experience calm.

On a country road in the still of night, you will find that silence invites a friendly spirit to speak to your heart and mind through words or feelings. Druantia resides among trees, so you'll receive spirit messages in a woodland setting. You may receive answers telepathically since you are receptive or can request guidance relating to any situation in the same way. The guidance may come instantly or later. Rest assured, spirit may be working silently to bring help, not deserting you.

Silence has many virtues. If someone has mistreated you, your silence is a source of strength without a word being spoken. Better than words, it reinforces your bold criticism of people's pitiless or selfish behavior. Silence is a form of wordless conversation to express your strong criticism. It is

better to be quiet than to speak or hear worthless or repetitive words that do not improve a relationship.

Something you put in writing may turn a situation in your favor. A new friend or lover will enter your life. You're about to discover friends who you feel comfortable with in silence, as opposed to those you don't. Your mind can absorb in quietness. You can also understand the psyche of the person you are with when you listen to what they have to say, before thinking of a reply.

Druantia's trees personify human life growing toward the light. When a tree is cut, it bleeds sap rather than blood and trees have a lifespan like people. As we grow from a seed to youth to maturity, so trees grow from a seed to a sapling to a mature tree, providing abundance for many forms of life. Trees have been our constant companions, supplying materials for homes, fires, tools, furniture, shoes, transport, and instruments. Tree bark, flowers, leaves, and fruits and nuts yield various remedies for many species. Without trees all creatures would die from a lack of oxygen. Tree roots relate to your personal tree of life, your family roots and tree. The trunk symbolizes your life's purpose and the energy you put into it. The branches denote you branching out, flowering, and fruitfulness.

The analogy between Druantia's silence and trees relates to kindness to yourself and others, and others to you. Kind words make you lovable, dissolve conflicts, and create confidence. Unexpected, kind, emotional, and physical rewards are heading your way. Be kind when you can as death can take away the chance to be kind to someone.

DRUANTIA'S MESSAGE Druantia's trees ask you to grow toward the light, going around any obstacles in your path. Stay rooted in your ancestry, among those who know you best. Don't be uprooted from your moral beliefs, but keep reaching higher like the branches of a tree. Your gifts will grow from your family roots and the spiritual seed of omniscience within you. When your mind is still, spirit will speak to you. Silence is a friend who never fails to show you the truth. Kindness will come by divine intervention as you're sympathetic without thought of reward.

DRUANTIA'S TREE PLANTING Plant a tree as a thank you to nature or to make a wish. As the tree grows, what you have aimed for will materialize.

DRUANTIA'S BAY LEAF FIDELITY DIVINATION To test a partner's fidelity, inscribe their name on a fresh laurel leaf with a pin. Put the leaf near your heart or under your pillow for a day. If it looks fresh, your partner is true. If it goes brown, they are not.

DRUANTIA'S LEAF SUPERSTITION A leaf blowing into your home foretells good news and wealth.

Andraste

GODDESS OF VICTORY

KEYWORDS: Eminence • Achievement • Rewards

COUNTRY OF ORIGIN: England

Andraste ensures you're nearer to victory than you envisage. When you conquer yourself, the victory belongs to you. Your efforts will be crowned with success as you are determined to succeed. Victory over yourself requires daily motivation. It is impossible to be victorious unless you persevere until your aim is achieved.

A problem will be resolved since you keep your mind flowing and enlightened through your own plans and God's plan for your life. You do not let a dilemma bog you down. Andraste's river fills gaps as it flows and uses the creative energy of time and nature. In the same way, you should deal with each stage of the situation you're trying to resolve since head-on efforts will see problems flow away, like the irreversible passage of time represented by Andraste's river.

Even when other people undermine your beliefs, you'll feel the elation of victory since you rise to meet the challenges of greater responsibilities. This gives you impressive power. Follow your heart and conscience, and do not fear what people think. Dedication to your purpose and spiritual strength will increase your confidence in winning. A friend will take you under their wing and protect you with words of advice, encouragement, and inspiration as well as practical help.

Your strength to resist temptation is a victory. Andraste's bay leaf crown signifies renewal, eternal life, and peace after defeating an enemy, whether this is an earthly battle or yourself in your attempts at self-improvement. Bay is ruled astrologically by the sun, and denotes cleansing the soul of guilt to bring bright, happy days ahead.

By having courage and the wisdom to walk the path of light, your journey will bring wealth, health, love, happiness, illumination, and other riches, as indicated by Andraste's golden sandals. When you're on the right path, keep going, even through difficulties. There is no internal or external problem you can't rise above, as shown by Andraste's wings. It's time to focus on the things you want which will change life for the better. Have faith in your ability to get the promotion or pay rise you ask for. You're on your way up while someone else is on their way down.

Take the plunge and ask someone for a meeting or date. Your disposition becomes happier and so too do your circumstances. Love-light is illuminating your love life, making something amazing happen. An attractive person will reveal their true intentions to you. As what you think, say, and do are in sync, you feel happy and more happiness will arrive through your actions.

If you're dedicated to your goal, you'll keep trying.

ANDRASTE'S MESSAGE If you're dedicated to your goal, you'll keep trying. Since you never give up, victory is possible. Try your hardest every day to achieve little victories and get the most out of what you have to give. The most challenging victory is achieving self-control. Every temptation that you resist is self-victory. The rewards of victory elevate you and make you feel good about yourself. No problem is insurmountable when you have the courage to face and deal with it.

ANDRASTE'S WISHING SPELL Use a pen to write your wish on a fresh or dry bay leaf. Light a candle. Hold the tip of the leaf to the flame. Say your wish aloud as the flame burns the leaf down to the stem. Drop the stem into a dish. Let the candle burn until you feel the time is right to snuff it out. Burn or bury the candle stub.

ANDRASTE'S SPELL TO ATTRACT VICTORY IN A GOAL OR REMOVE A PROBLEM Find a pebble. Clasp it in your hands while thinking of a victory you wish to achieve. Or, while clasping the pebble, think of a problem you wish to be rid of. Throw the pebble into a river. Walk away from the river without looking back.

ANDRASTE'S BAY LEAF "YES" OR "NO" DIVINATION Clasp a bay leaf in your hands while concentrating on your question. Drop the leaf into a fire. If the leaf burns brightly, the answer is "yes." If it smolders, the answer is "no."

Cessair

GODDESS OF COURAGE

KEYWORDS: Willpower • Knowledge • Activity

COUNTRY OF ORIGIN: Ireland

Cessair, supreme goddess of knowledge, willpower, and activity, blesses nature with healthy crops and promotes dedication and courage in you. You're stronger than you think and capable of resolving a difficulty stage by stage. You embody heavenly higher powers on Earth, making you courageous and determined to succeed. You will gain freedom by having the bravery to overcome the fear of failure, follow your heartfelt intuition, and achieve your dreams, so they have a chance of coming true. Weed out the negative people or thoughts in your life.

The vegetables presided over by Cessair indicate that your optimism is the root of your progress, as you push through barriers to keep moving forward. Vegetation grows from seeds in the earth. Even in your darkest times, forces of light within you will push through the obstruction of winter to become life-giving in spring. These seeds represent your soul growing from darkness into the light. Your courage to keep faith and push for justice will give you strength and inspire others. The more courageous you are, the more resilient you'll become. You'll look back and see that you survived a testing time by facing trouble with fortitude, trial with modesty and patience, and disappointment with optimism. Your

past trials and tribulations will reward you, making you better equipped to cope with problems.

Find the courage to stop someone holding you back from pursuing your destiny. You can overcome numerous difficulties when you apply your intention and use your willpower, which grows stronger with use. You have the wisdom to know when courage becomes stupidity, that an excess of fortitude is foolish, and the risk you take must be governed by being sensible and divine law.

Just as Cessair blesses agriculture, nourishment, and wealth, you'll find that what you're doing meets with good fortune, success, and prosperity. A relationship will be long-lasting, as you've secured its foundation on moral principles of trust and devotion. You may get a new home with a present partner and have children. You are at the beginning of something new that holds the seeds for potential success. Nourish the seeds and they will grow. You appreciate what you have and build on it to have more. In work, now is the time to ask for a pay rise or perhaps a promotion. If you apply for a new job, you will get it. Good health will help you keep on top of duties and resolutions. As you become happier, so do your circumstances. Unusual chances that bring breakthroughs are imminent, as you have sown the seeds for them to see the light of day. Your search for a higher purpose will bring rich spiritual and physical rewards.

CESSAIR'S MESSAGE You're strengthened to face adversity fearlessly as the light of supreme illumination is growing like a seed within you. Heavenly light blesses your plans with divine intelligence, esoteric knowledge, spiritual persistence, and the fruits of your determination. Ask each day for a miracle to happen; little ones will occur. Given time, like a growing seed, a surprise miracle will appear.

CESSAIR'S SPELLS FOR COURAGE

- Hot mustard seeds are ruled by the fire planet Mars. Soak absorbent cotton (cotton wool) in water and place it in a dish. Sprinkle mustard seeds on top, while saying: *"I am strong and courageous. As these seeds grow, so shall my seeds of courage and strength within me grow."* Place the dish near the sink. When you look at the growing seeds, your courage will be reinforced. A week later, to absorb Mars' fighting spirit, cut the stalks and eat them. Bury the absorbent cotton.

- Myrrh is also ruled by the planet Mars. Rub myrrh oil from the tip of a long candle to midway. Turn the candle upside down and rub more oil from the base to midway. If you're using a tealight, rub the oil on the wax around the wick. Light the candle while saying: *"I can face this event [name the event]. I will face this event [name the event]. And I will have success at this event [name the event]."* Let the candle burn to a stub or snuff it out when it's nearly there.

Flidais

GODDESS OF TRAVEL

KEYWORDS: Flight • Carefree • Exploration

COUNTRY OF ORIGIN: Ireland

New roads to success are opening up for you. You'll visit new locations for work, pleasure, or both. Your road to this success is being constructed daily and there are sometimes repairs to be made. You're moving through a testing time, for which you are still searching for a meaning. Keep forging ahead on a new pathway, stay focused, and avoid distractions because you will eventually reach your destination, as symbolized by Flidais who built highways and rode a chariot pulled by deer. Her chariot is an analogy for your body, which is the vehicle that carries your spirit through life. You will find the missing part of yourself and feel whole again, as symbolized by the antlers of deer which annually regrow when shed. Like a deer, you will leap elegantly over obstacles.

Flidais rules forests, woodlands, and wild beasts. The forests and woods are the untamed part of your nature, which may need reining in if you are to go forward unencumbered. But your self-reliance will keep your life on track. Just keep moving forward and don't look back. You'll discover more about yourself by traveling into the wilderness of your inner self. Hunters stalk their prey in woods, so always question peoples' motives and avoid being someone's victim.

A vacation or new car is forecast. A new project will succeed due to persistent hard work. You're moving away from problems by taking control and finding solutions. You'll break out of a rut by meeting someone who can help you. Their knowledge and connections will help you reach your destination faster. A person you are fond of will contact you for a beneficial meeting or reunion where you will gain knowledge. This may lead to a relationship that brings fun into your life.

Through God-given talents you'll keep learning and exploring possibilities that fulfill your hunger for knowledge and expression. Now is the time to get involved in groups that you're interested in. By developing different facets of your nature, you'll become more powerful and love something you discover for the first time. An appealing change will help you find new social or work opportunities.

A subject you research will further your development and broaden your horizons. If you're fearful about an appointment, tell yourself that you can't wait to get there. Your apprehension is holding you back from something that is not as bad as you think. You are starting out on a new path that enhances your self-discovery and the lives of those you meet. You are on a journey to change and

You are starting out on a new path that enhances your self-discovery and the lives of those you meet.

renewal. You are leaving behind a rough and rocky road to enjoy new-found independence and freedom from constraints. Crossing your path is an adventure you would do well to take if its foundation is morally right.

FLIDAIS'S MESSAGE Think only good thoughts as they can travel and affect others. Your adventurous spirit knows you should turn around if you're not on the right track. Your vision isn't blurred, so you can overcome anything and possess the freedom to be whatever you wish. You'll discover that your great ability to forgive unblocks your pathway to happiness, so you can travel lightly.

FLIDAIS'S SPELLS FOR TRAVEL

- Focus on the picture of Flidais. Now light a votive candle and place it on a table. Close your eyes and visualize where you would like to visit. Imagine the place as vividly as you can. Let the candle keep burning or snuff it out.
- Cut out pictures of the place you'd like to visit and words that name the location. Paste a picture of yourself in the center of a large piece of paper and the travel pictures around your photo. Draw arrows from your photo to the pictures. Under the pictures write words such as: *"I will travel to [name of place]"* and *"I will holiday in [name of place]."* Keep the paper where you will see it often or out of sight. When your wish has been fulfilled, burn or bury the piece of paper. Don't throw the paper away, as this would be like throwing yourself in the garbage.

Morgan le Fay

GODDESS OF SORCERY

KEYWORDS: Temptation • Power • Unrequited love

COUNTRY OF ORIGIN: England

You may feel you are being tested to abandon right for wrong or to give up faith and self-belief. Be careful not to expose yourself to needless danger. Like a wolf, you need to outsmart someone who seems harmless, but could turn on you when you fall into their trap. You'll see through someone and an attempt to discover another person's secrets will reveal your intuition to be correct. The symbolism of Morgan le Fay's wolf, a faithful guardian of a person's spirit, shows you can trust that spiritual forces are protecting you. A person who pursues others for sexual gratification, help, or money may try to seduce you. You know who this person is.

A long period of success will follow a short phase of unhappiness. You will earn enough to pay your way by being alert to business opportunities and cautious with spending. Prosperous times will return in your very near future. Someone who helps you will become a reliable friend, worker, and advisor. A new line of work will be successful from the outset. Your efforts to attain a better position will be rewarded as you're channeling your energy to achieve your aim.

If you're broken-hearted in love, that person may try to reunite with you. But the reason for the split will still exist if you rekindle the passion. Giving money or gifts will not buy love. You're now in a position to test a past relationship and one you have yet to discover. You can choose to move on or settle for what you know. If the lover from the past doesn't pursue you, they have left you behind. Neither your past lover nor the new person will ever meet anyone as unique as you.

An adventurous time lies ahead. A new friend has good advice that should not be ignored. You'll receive good news from relatives and a rift will be healed. A family invitation will benefit you. Help will come when needed. Being kind to someone who has hurt you will melt their heart. Morgan le Fay was King Arthur's greatest enemy, but they were reconciled, so resolve family differences. Morgan le Fay, Merlin's apprentice, channeled her magic, which shows you can direct what you need by requesting it, believing it will arrive, and aiming for it. Put your supernatural powers to good use. Morgan le Fay's sadness is due to her unrequited love for Lancelot. In such a situation, live your life with a new admirer who offers true love and much more. Don't get stuck in the past or lose heart. Not getting what you want could be lucky. A divine power may deliver you from unseen adversities to a prize that will bless you with more happiness than you can imagine.

MORGAN LE FAY'S MESSAGE Life is presenting you with several good surprises. Your life today is a combination of your past, appreciating your present, and creating a good future. Much of your future good fortune is within your control. Being a sorceress, you can manifest a great deal of what happens by ensuring that good things take place and reacting well and positively to whatever comes your way.

MORGAN LE FAY'S SPELL TO HEAL UNREQUITED LOVE Friday night is the best time for this spell since the day is ruled by Venus, the planet of love. The night of a full moon is good because as the moon wanes, so will your heartache.

Using a pen, write lengthwise on a long candle the name of the person who has caused heartache. Smear the candle with rose oil from the top to midway and from the base to midway. Light the candle, look at the flame, and say: *"[Name of person], my broken heart is healing. My heart and mind are free from feelings and thoughts of you. I am free."* Take another long candle and smear with lavender oil in the same way. Lavender is ruled by the planet Mercury, which speeds communication. Put the candle beside the first candle, then light it and say: *"I am over you [name of person who broke your heart]. I attract a partner much better suited to me."* Without spilling the wax, move the second candle away from the first over an evening, to symbolically distance yourself from the person you named. Let both candles burn to a stub or snuff them out near to the base. Bury the stubs.

Guinevere

GODDESS OF MARRIAGE

KEYWORDS: Fidelity • Fascination • Passion

COUNTRY OF ORIGIN: Wales

Stay true to yourself, as faithfulness is sacred. The goddess Guinevere alludes to fidelity in a relationship since infidelity causes chaos. Plans, dreams, and ambitions will only go out of sync when you do something that you know you shouldn't. Irresistible, evil trickery often appears disguised as good. By resisting temptation, you can overcome it. Your own insight gives you wisdom if you look deeply within and test your power through your ability to do the right thing. Temptation reveals who you are to yourself and others. If you don't see the light, you weaken heavenly help and divine influence by disconnecting yourself from their power.

Guinevere's crown alludes to "the crown of life" that a person receives when they resist temptation. Sincerity and fidelity are the highest sacred good. Queen Guinevere lost her crown after an affair with Lancelot, her husband King Arthur's chief knight and friend, and lived the rest of her days repenting in a convent. Fidelity is a choice of the soul. Guinevere did not show fidelity, so lost her husband and kingdom. Her soul did not remain strong when tested by temptation, which came in the form of love. Guinevere loved Lancelot too much to resist. Your love life holds the seeds of many good things, as symbolized by the multiseeded pomegranate, an ancient multicultural symbol of conjugal love, fidelity, marriage, life, and rebirth.

You are making a strong connection with a soul mate—your knight in shining armor who may be someone you know, have spoken to but not yet met, or a love-at-first-sight meeting that is days or weeks away. One pomegranate seed bears a new tree and lots of fruit. Meeting the right person correlates to one seed magically bringing seasons of happiness, beauty, and variety into your life.

Make the most of abundant opportunities, as highlighted by Guinevere's fertile tree of apples which signify ancestral wisdom and a thirst for knowledge. Like a family tree, you're branching out into prosperity and growth, bearing fruit in love and ambition. If you let people know what you want, it seems you'll get it. The apples relate to materialistic desires. You'll feather your nest financially and settle with a loved one. The tree has its roots in the ground and branches in the air, which shows you're midway between earthly desires and pure spirituality—you can have both and your success will be visible. One or many of your ideas have great financial potential and you'll have an opportunity to rise in status. In your career and personal ambition, your persuasive

power is strong. Push yourself before the sun sets on your aspirations.

You will have renewed peace of mind as you mix progress and pleasure with important, helpful people. You'll have a crowning achievement with a far-reaching effect. Guinevere's wisdom gave her foresight and made her the counselor goddess. She helped heroes worthy of esteem and was kind in peace and war. Similarly, you stay loyal to the people you care about who you advise and help. Perhaps someone's partner has been unfaithful, but keeping their secret is a sign of fidelity. You'll enjoy feeling trusted, and your loyalty will be rewarded.

GUINEVERE'S MESSAGE Guinevere's doomed love affair with Lancelot began when she fell in love with temptation. This started the disintegration of the Round Table and Arthur's Kingdom. True, genuine, heartfelt love means putting a loved one's happiness before your own. True love within you helps you discover a hidden beauty in loyalty which is a test of your faithfulness. Your nearest and dearest value and respect your loyalty, truthfulness, and tact. Loyalty is what you decide in your soul, knowing it brings self-respect and honor to those who trust you.

GUINEVERE'S SPELL TO WIN THE HEART OF THE ONE YOU LOVE Inscribe the name of the one you love lengthwise with a pin on a long, white candle, from top to bottom. Inscribe your name on the other side. Place the candle in a holder and light it. Speak to the flame as if it is the person you love. Let the candle burn through both names, then either leave it to burn out or snuff it out. Bury the candle stub.

Caolainn

GODDESS OF WISDOM

KEYWORDS: Experience • Acumen • Expectation

COUNTRY OF ORIGIN: Ireland.

Caolainn, who cured her own wounds, alludes to you having the power to free yourself from suffering and to treat your body and spirit healthily. Her stars mean celestial help is there for you to call upon for any emotional, health, or physical predicament—your problems will be solved, as people will offer to help you. You're wiser now and will continue to be since your past has taught you many things. You learn wisdom through thinking, experience, and emulating other people's qualities. Every adversity contains a seed of wisdom that helps you overcome present struggles. Your religion and spirituality stand you in good stead.

You're determined to succeed and behave as you wish to appear. You are wise enough to do what is right and act on advice while keeping your own counsel. A foolish person refuses good advice. You're prudent enough to make your own decisions and to take responsibility for your future, while creating opportunities for yourself. A humbling event has made you see reality more clearly, making you optimistic that life is getting better and people wish you well.

You are self-aware and know when to stop doing anything that might harm your well-being. You can cooperate with many different people as you wisely listen to them and talk less. You know first appearances can be deceptive and that wisdom is an attribute which keeps you away from dilemmas. Your intelligence stops you being anyone's enemy or victim, or wishing misfortune on those who hurt you. Your forgiveness upsets your enemies, encouraging them to wish you well and offer practical help. A secret is being revealed to you by someone. Keep that secret and realize you would be foolish to expect other people to.

Your own situation is being healthily revived. A new beginning is heading your way, so be prepared for a change of fortune in your current circumstances. A bad situation is quickly ending to release you from stress and restriction. If you have to make a choice, the omen is that you'll make the right one and also attain your spiritual destiny. You will receive messages of reassurance from departed loved ones and divine forces confirming that you're not alone, but have their heavenly help to make your wishes come true. Ask them for what you need to be granted and they will magically speed it to you. The right connections are heading your way. You have a strong willpower and personality, and the power to control yourself from without and from within, so increasing your insight. More than one person is in love with you since you are good-natured. Your good nature is drawn from the well of life, which gives you wisdom. Water has no shape, meaning the potential is there for you to create the life force within you by motivating your personality to keep going forward. Water is constantly active—below ground, it forms springs, rivers, wells, and seas. Above ground, it produces rain and dew. You are heading in a positive direction.

CAOLAINN'S MESSAGE You have the ability to gain intuitive wisdom from past experience and from wise people who set a good example. You have it within the depths of your being to aim high and head for your star guiding you to fulfill your preordained destiny. You'll never wallow in a muddy swamp because, like water, you do a multitude of good. Water never struggles; it wears away what is hard and flows along a natural path to get to where it needs to be.

SHOOTING STAR OMENS

- Make a wish on seeing a shooting star, as it is believed to have magical powers.
- A shooting star on your right means good luck will befall you, and "yes" to a question you've asked. A shooting star on your left means misfortune or a problematic situation is leaving you, and "no" to a question you've asked.
- On seeing a shooting star, tie a knot in your handkerchief or clothing to bind good luck to you. Or pick up a stone and keep it for good luck.
- Seeing lots of stars in one night or over a few nights foretells great happiness.

Ragnall
GODDESS OF GRATITUDE

KEYWORDS: Thankfulness • Honor • Plenty

COUNTRY OF ORIGIN: England

Ragnall, goddess of gratitude, foretells that you are about to enjoy a well-deserved, carefree time when responsibilities and hard work are less prominent since you've dealt with them already. You are going to experience a brilliant period and thank your lucky stars, as symbolized by Ragnall's diadem crown which represents commitment. By conquering yourself you are crowned with eternal victory in life and the afterlife. Aligned in the stars, heaven-sent magic is shining rays of spiritual enlightenment on your hopes and dreams, so you rise above what has been and reach your highest everyday happiness and aspirations.

You have been challenged by obstacles and battled against the odds, as represented by Ragnall's hill. Now you have made it to the top of the hill, you have a panoramic view in perspective and the walk is easier. Your sense of humor has lifted your spirits and lessened the tension during hard times when you kept going. Having worked hard to get what you want, you are thankful you've now got it. Your gratitude has turned an unsatisfying situation into a positive because you are more appreciative of what you may have taken for granted. Many pleasant love and career possibilities that have been closed to you will now open up. If

you're looking for love, you may suddenly meet a special someone who becomes your lover since you possess the key of laughter to their heart.

Your spirit is getting stronger and your higher principles, ruling over lower desires, provide continuous improvements to your material needs and emotional happiness. Ragnall revealed oracles, and the sacred mystery that gratitude is needed for happiness. The more you show gratitude, the more you'll magnetically attract and multiply earthly and heavenly things to be thankful for. When you count your blessings, abundance appears and doubt disappears. You will feel dissatisfied and never have enough if you dwell on what you haven't got. If you don't treasure what you have, it's wasted and you're less likely to attract more. When you're thankful more blessings will appear and you'll notice miracles every day that look coincidental or come along at the right time. The more often you thank, the more often you will get.

By feeling happy, you keep your vibration higher, so you naturally make those around you happy too. Show someone appreciation to brighten their day and make a difference to their life.

You're now ahead of the game, having encouraged good fortune and turned a situation into

You'll have a crowning achievement of success through your spiritual enlightenment

financial, romantic, and physical reality. Seeing all you've strived and wished for coming true will boost your confidence, bringing acclaim from beyond your immediate circle of family and friends. Expect applause and appreciation which will open new doors, leading you to pastures new where you sit in comfort and peace of mind. Emotionally and financially you will have much happiness and fulfillment to be thankful for. Your lightened mood is bringing you spontaneous tears of laughter that are infectious. Other people will appreciate your laughter as it may remedy their sadness. They too can be a thankful recipient and reap an abundant harvest.

RAGNALL'S MESSAGE You'll have a crowning achievement of success through your spiritual enlightenment, knowing that showing gratitude brings blessings of good fortune. You're blessed when you happily give and thankfully receive. Be grateful for what you have and work to get what you want—complaining will only reinforce what you haven't got. Laughter lightens your mood, so you look at things from a higher perspective and see the gratitude magic working. If someone is mean with money, rest assured that deep down they are mean-spirited. Practical help is given reluctantly rather than with a willing heart.

RAGNALL'S SPELL FOR A NEW JOB OR MORE MONEY Put a bay leaf in each shoe and one in your purse (especially before a job interview). Keep the leaves there for one day, then bury them in your backyard or scatter in the park or countryside.

Cailleach

GODDESS OF MIRACLES

KEYWORDS: Anticipation • Belief • Tenacity

COUNTRY OF ORIGIN: Scotland

You are being released from hard times, perhaps a season of despair, painful experiences, loneliness, sadness, heartache, remorse, or physical affliction, as symbolized by Cailleach, Queen of Winter and Witch of Ben Cruachan and springtime gales known as "A'Chailleach." Always keeping her promise that spring will come, Cailleach shows this is a time when divinity will send you a spectacular miracle. This will stand out in the landscape of your life as clearly as Ben Nevis, the tallest mountain of the British Isles and Cailleach's throne.

Cailleach advocates never giving up and believing you can achieve your soul's yearning. In the bleakness of winter spring is veiled and unseen, but starting the blooming process. Fabulous creations bringing fresh inspiration can even come from disaster, just as Scotland's Loch Awe sprang from an overflowing mountain spring beside which, exhausted, Cailleach fell asleep while deer-herding.

Cailleach, or "veiled one," is a wise old woman and witch, who shows you have the wisdom to laugh at impossibilities and see they can become possibilities. Self-possessed and with good judgment during stormy challenges, you view matters from a higher perspective while climbing a mountain to its

peak—Earth's closest point to Heaven. Like Cailleach on her throne, you have panoramic vision.

The warm enclosure of Cailleach's cloak, a talisman that surrounds her aura, indicates you are protected and have cocooned yourself in dignity and kindness, overlapped with mystery, enchantment, and nature. You avoid danger on your journey, which involves mind, body, and spiritual changes. Traveling light, you carry the essence of parental-taught, childhood values into adult life, which helps you take a firm stand, as shown by Cailleach's standing stones. These represent Bodach, Cailleach's husband, and their children beside a small shelter—known as Tigh nan Cailliche (old woman's home)—in the Glen of Loch Lyon, Perthshire.

Cailleach's deer, spiritual messengers exemplifying intuitive authority, who stare in response to your behavior and hide to keep safe, suggest you're experiencing a mystic awakening. Good news, luck, success, wealth, marriage, happiness, and a sincere love partner (if single) will be revealed. Like deer antlers that fall to regrow, your life is being regenerated.

You see calmly from your elevated perspective when storm clouds gather, seemingly obscuring you overcoming obstacles and progressing to your

mountain top. You may have no idea how matters will turn out, but know that the clouds shall pass. Things will turn out well when you remain seated on your throne, close to Heaven and divine revelations. Clouds, which are heavenly in origin, bring celestial prophecies and fertility to the land, meaning they are not to be feared. Good will come, as clouds are always metamorphozing into visionary images, helping you to look up, rise above the tedious, and receive out-of-this-world divinations and more than one miracle in your life. Your life's experiences and acquired knowledge make you a wise woman or man. In future, you'll reflect on the good fortune that turned you into a wise one when you were young, before the time you may look like an old hag or storm-witch.

CAILLEACH'S MESSAGE The rewards you attain when achieving your aim lift your spirit and bring physical security and a wonderful panorama. You can weather a storm, retain your serenity, and enjoy being wind-tossed when celestial forces and divine revelations propel things in different directions. Elevated above mundane everyday existence, you're progressing to the top of the world. The winds of change are sending a well-deserved, heaven-sent miracle to you.

CAILLEACH'S "YES" OR "NO" DIVINATION
Arrange stones in a bowl shape, higher at the rim than the hollow center. Throw a stone at the pile while asking a "yes" or "no" question. If the stone lands and stays in the pile, the answer is "yes," but if it lands on the rim or doesn't land on the pile at all, the answer is "no."

Igraine

GODDESS OF RESPECT

KEYWORDS: Dignity • Esteem • Preference

COUNTRY OF ORIGIN: England

You will do something important and perhaps life-changing for someone close to you who needs your help since they don't have the strength or finances to cope at the moment. The person may be a relative for whom you're willing to give something up through the necessity of love. For their dignity and well-being, you may be spending less time on yourself, but it won't feel as if you're sacrificing anything. Your long-term happiness is influenced by what you decide to relinquish to achieve it. Like it or not, it is your duty to do certain things. Respect helps you tolerate doing what your conscience tells you must be done. Since you're kind your good actions are character-building. They make you well-loved, respected, and admired, inspiring other people to emulate your good qualities.

You may have to say "no" to a partner to care for a sibling or parent, as blood is thicker than water. If your partner doesn't honor your dutiful decision, then perhaps you should distance yourself from them and question whether they are self-absorbed. If a person truly loves you, they will respect your decision. Although you can't make someone respect you, you can take a break or leave if they don't.

You must stay strong to avoid accepting less than what is best for you. It would be wrong to lower your standards or compromise your principles to please someone who is blocking you. You will gain self-respect by doing what is right and also test how much your partner cares for you. Your challenges prepare you for greater things. In the same way, Igraine allowed her son, Arthur, to fulfill his higher calling by letting the wizard Merlin raise him. So, honor your commitment and relinquish something now to gain what you need for the rest of your life. You don't want to live with regret, so consider your aim and what you must commit to doing to achieve it. Like Igraine, you're in alignment when you surrender to your conscience, so the action you take is for the highest good of everyone involved.

With strength, courage, and patience Igraine took a leap of faith and released Arthur to achieve the long-term happiness of many, believing that Merlin could bring out his excellence. In her mind's eye, Igraine felt she could unlock Arthur's Kingdom as she knew that Merlin held the master key to unlocking his potential. You also hold the key to setting someone free and confining another who is trying to stop you fulfilling your destiny.

Merlin taught Arthur herbal medicine, swordsmanship, and how to read the stars. In a Westminster church a magical sword in a stone bore

*You must stay strong to avoid accepting
less than what is best for you.*

the inscription: "Whoso pulleth out this sword from this stone is right wise king born of all England." Only Arthur could draw the sword from the stone and so was crowned King of England and the Round Table and united the people of Ireland, Scotland, Wales, and England against Saxon invaders. Arthur's sword symbolizes that you have the power to defend someone and the forces of light against the dark. Love wins over affliction. You can save someone's life and their lifestyle.

IGRAINE'S MESSAGE By giving up something for a loved one or what you really care about, you achieve more for the greater good of yourself and others. You respect your family's opinions and avoid demeaning another's dignity. Since your conduct and principles are based on respect and kindness, you honor your commitment. Love, sympathy, justice, and forgiveness are your good traits. Spirit will appear to you through everyday people who answer a call in miraculous ways.

IGRAINE'S SPELL FOR LOVE TO STAY Take strands of hair from your lover's hairbrush or comb and from your own. Tie the strands together. Focus on the picture of Igraine. Light a pink candle, look at the flame, and say: *"[Name of person], I bind you to me in love."* Put the hair in a new envelope or one given to you by your lover. Let the candle burn before snuffing it out. Sleep with the envelope under your pillow or keep it among your possessions. To reverse the spell, bury or burn the envelope with the hair.

Enid

GODDESS OF LOYALTY

KEYWORDS: Constant • Faithful • Dedication

COUNTRY OF ORIGIN: Wales

Be loyal to yourself, listen to your conscience and spirit within, and recognize signs as messages that guide you. Follow your dreams even when other people try to distract you. Enid's name means "spirit life, soul purity" and also "bread." The epitome of feminine virtue, Enid was loyal to her husband, helped defend borders from invasion, and their marriage was happy. Like bread, loyalty and purity are the staff of life, fueling and sustaining you. The analogy means you should cultivate loyal and pure soul decisions as those are best for your happiness. Being loyal or self-sacrificing to an unworthy cause is not beneficial, so don't be coerced and betrayed by disloyal people befriending you. Consider who you are loyal to, so your loyalty is not misplaced or betrayed.

The good people you are with recognize you to be trustworthy, as you're not disloyal to absent people. Confidentiality is your virtue and you will learn much from people who recognize your self-respect, and trust you to hear their problems and keep their secrets. Your loyalty is what makes others trust, stay, hope, and feel secure. Through you they see that people cannot be both loyal and disloyal.

Do not allow someone with vices to come between you and someone you love who is more worthwhile. In a dilemma, when you don't know what to think, give your loyalty to the deserving who have been loyal to you, not to someone whose loyalty you have yet to test. Like Enid's dog, which represents faithfulness, you won't abandon people who need the loyalty that lies deep within you. Enid's lilies symbolize the beauty of visible and sweet-scented loyalty. When upset, don't get angry, but instead be like the damaged, delicate little flower. When you believe that your hopes will blossom, then you'll be rewarded by heaven-sent opportunities which you could never have planned for. Whatever direction you are moving in, you're on the ascent. Loyalty to your principles makes everything easier.

Just as Enid was pursued by suitors due to her beauty, so will you. A current partner will be very loving, taking commitment to the next level. If unattached, you may cross paths with your soul mate. A new job, promotion, or better paid work is imminent. You may move to a new home or hear of an addition to your family. You may conceive and give birth to a healthy baby. Make the most of the present moment, as you are freed from restrictions.

Travel is showing you new possibilities. You have every reason to look forward with hope to a venture being successful and have better prospects than ever in health, prosperity, and freedom of choice. You're wise to be loyal, as being faithful to your goals and nearest and dearest makes you happy and improves other people's lives. Faithfulness creates an uplifting chemistry for you and the receiver, lightening and healing yours and other people's loads. Faithful people are the nicest to know and being one of them, you can change someone's day by genuinely listening to what they are saying and responding with loyal integrity.

ENID'S MESSAGE You realize fidelity is important in all relationships and are selflessly there for people who need your help. Your enthusiasm rekindles the flame of hope when you're called upon for assistance. You're purifying your thinking. People to whom you are loyal may not be loyal to you in return. To protect yourself, withdraw from draining people and cultivate those who will help you as much as you help them. Someone needs you to nourish them financially or emotionally, or with advice. Your pride and self-respect mean that you are turning away from your own weaknesses and being faithful to a worthy cause.

ENID'S SPELL FOR A WISH TO BE FULFILLED

On top of a table, place a shell with a red candle on either side. Light the candles, then tell the flames what you would like to happen. Let the candles burn out or snuff them out. Keep the shell as an amulet. Hold the shell to your ear and you may hear the sound of the sea as well as the answer to a question.

Marcia Proba

GODDESS OF JUSTICE

KEYWORDS: Integrity • Virtue • Fairness

COUNTRY OF ORIGIN: England

Marcia Proba's name means "virtuous and upright." Like her, your virtue is an outward expression of your inner soul. When things are not harmonious you feel unsettled and unhappy. Your conscience and sense of justice ensure fairness in the decisions you make. Every choice has a consequence. Your good deeds and intentions result in immediate and future happiness, while your bad decisions cause immediate or future suffering. Right choices automatically bring rewards since justice results from choice and action. In the spirit world, justice is on your side as everything has a divine intention behind it. You'll find your life's purpose by adhering to the divine law and doing what is right according to your conscience, even when you don't want to. This means treating people well and doing the right thing, even when they are undeserving of your fairness.

A love interest or joint business venture will be good for both of you. If you're footloose, someone you're attracted to will say "yes" to a date, bringing you fulfillment and mutual agreement. If your life is out of balance, you have the strength to rebalance it. If you've fallen out with someone and been accused of behaving badly, you'll be judged sympathetically, even if you've done something wrong and regret your mistake. If you're trying to lose weight, kick a bad habit, or better balance your finances, you'll find the strength to succeed, as you're in the right frame of mind and this grows stronger daily. Your well-balanced words, thoughts, and actions make good things happen at the right time. Self-discipline and forgiveness create harmony. You're giving time to those you love, so you have harmony in your life. You live in peace, fairness, and agreement with yourself, creating balance in all your deeds and relationships and the universe.

Marcia Proba's evergreen laurel crown represents your immortal soul. Daily effort, forgiveness, and giving of your best are needed for continued success. It is the crown of winners, riches, stardom, peace, victory, and triumph over conflict. You can achieve all you set your heart and soul on, as divine justice puts you in the right place at the right time. External justice comes from harmonious psychic motion within you, revealing the path that destiny has mapped out for you. Be in union with your conscience and you'll have equilibrium and stability in your physical life. People who have doubted you, or failed to support you, will see you achieve huge success in your endeavors.

*If you've fallen out with someone and been accused of behaving badly,
you'll be judged sympathetically.*

MARCIA PROBA'S MESSAGE You possess the energy to push things forward by gaining a deeper and kinder understanding of yourself. You're balancing your work and pleasure time better, reprioritizing, and using good judgment in tricky situations. You'll have good relationships with people you may have fallen out with, which will bring happiness as you find a fair answer to a difficult dilemma. If you're involved in a legal situation or dispute with a trading company, negotiating fairly and approaching a higher authority will bring the result you want by lending weight to your side. What you presently say and do affects your future success.

MARCIA PROBA'S SPELL FOR LEGAL SUCCESS OR JUSTICE To win a legal matter, put the legal letters in an envelope. Sprinkle camphor oil over the envelope. Take an ice-cube tray and sprinkle three drops of oil into each section. On a small piece of paper, write: *"I will win this legal dispute with [name of company]."* Put the paper in one of the sections. Slowly fill each section with water and put the tray in the freezer. On the night of a full moon, empty all the ice cubes into a bowl to melt. Place the bowl in front of a white candle and light the candle. Say: *"As this candle burns, light is illuminating strength on my side to win this legal dispute with [name of company]. This legal dispute will dissolve and resolve in my favor."* Once the cubes have melted and the candle burned to a stub, snuff the candle out. Bury the paper and pour the water in the bowl over it. As the paper disintegrates and the full moon wanes, so too will your legal dispute and you will win.

Aerten

GODDESS OF PEACE

KEYWORDS: Rest • Tranquillity • Freedom

COUNTRY OF ORIGIN: Wales

Aerten presides over the successful outcome of war. Her axe, a symbol of light, divine power, and celestial illumination, suggests you should cut the deadwood from your life and sever links with the people or situations causing you inner conflict. Being double-edged, Aerten's axe cuts both ways, which means that unforeseen results may rebound on you should you verbally attack or speak your mind strongly to someone rather than reasoning with them. Keep the peace by considering the consequences that voicing your opinion could have in the future.

You can be the person you'll be happy to live with for the rest of your life. You are promised peace of mind and precious pearls of wisdom, which you'll treasure. Self-contentment need not depend on circumstances. Money is bringing happiness and freedom, but cannot be enjoyed without peace of mind. If there is friction around you, handle conflicts calmly to shake off negative feelings that threaten your equilibrium. You avoid warring with yourself and find peace by having love, not hate, in your heart. You know letting go of angry thoughts brings tranquillity, enabling you to cope with difficult situations and manage conflicts fairly.

Aerten's doves symbolize your soul and peace. This means that by grasping the truth you will resolve a situation peacefully rather than attacking or defending with sharp words. You have the strength to remain calm under stress and also a peaceful heart in the midst of troubles. Calm will prevail through a difficult situation and keeping the end result peaceful will bring serenity. Calmness creates right thinking and actions, which lead to peace of mind when battling problems and setbacks, and you'll be less unsettled by these. You'll stay centered rather than harmed. You're winning the war by awakening yourself to a higher presence and resisting the temptation to be hostile to yourself and others. You'll settle a situation peacefully when you know that higher forces are assisting you.

Aerten's pairs of doves and axe represent the war between body and spirit, indicating that a difficult ordeal is now behind you. Arguments and self-conflict will end successfully. Those who've upset you will feel ashamed and react by treating you better. The head of Aerten's axe, similar in shape to a cross, shows you're at a crossroads. The innocence symbolized by the doves will lead to honor and prosperity when you choose peace not war. That doesn't mean you shouldn't defend what is rightfully yours. Your inner tranquillity comes from being kind to people, even when they don't deserve it. You rise above adversity

by keeping a sense of humor, so that troubles loosen their hold over you. You can overcome a painful situation more easily when you have inner calm, so your thoughts don't conflict. You resolve not to let other people undermine your peace of mind and know your happiness will soar to new heights, as if on the wings of a dove.

AERTEN'S MESSAGE Heaven is helping you reconnect with your spirituality. When your higher self rules, heaven-sent physical and emotional rewards appear. Don't entertain guilt or fear; let calmness prevail and so live more peacefully. Your time is better spent battling for peace, not conflict. Don't let other people destroy your inner peace. It is much easier to live with yourself and others when there is peace.

AERTEN'S RECONCILIATION SPELL Using a pen, write on a white candle the name of the person you wish to reconcile with. Light the candle and talk to the flame as if you're speaking to that person. Write your name on another white candle. Light the candle and place both candle holders so they are touching. Let the candles burn until you want to snuff them out. Place the stubs in an envelope and bury them.

WHITE DOVE OMENS White doves are a sign that the spirit of heaven is with you and an omen of happiness in love. To see white doves fly is an omen of success in a feud. A white dove in front of you signifies happiness in love and, if you are single, a new romantic lover who could be the one intended for you.

Maeve

GODDESS OF SEDUCTION

KEYWORDS: Enticement • Allure • Charm

COUNTRY OF ORIGIN: Ireland

One of the strongest Irish fighting forces, Maeve, who symbolizes power over men, is said to be buried in Knocknarea, County Sligo, Ireland. A king could not be crowned without the royal ceremony being consummated in Maeve's bed. The analogy is that you must not allow yourself to be sweet-talked into a deceitful business deal or led astray in love. Your sensuality is igniting passion in someone who wants to seduce you. Lust, not a long-term relationship, may be inflaming their passion. Or a person may use seduction to sidetrack you from what you should be doing or lead you astray from someone you should be loyal to.

Someone pretending to be in love with you might be grooming you for money or some other gain. An enticing, but corrupt, offer may come, encouraging you to invest in a fraudulent company. Evil's greatest destructive tool is deception, which can be attractively disguised. Maeve's pitcher of mead represents the intoxication of love that can make a person behave irrationally. Neurochemicals, including dopamine, course through a person's body when they're in love, which means they may behave out of character. You may be charming and appealing yourself and use your sexuality as a tool to make someone help you.

Maeve's warriors fought fervently for her. If someone is truly in love with you, they'll want to win your heart, not just your body. You're becoming mentally closer to someone you know by delving into a deeper part of their psyche. You are highly principled in love, aware that it doesn't mean someone is in love with you just because you're not sleeping with anyone but them. You can wage war against seduction by getting to know a person before sleeping with them. Loving someone is different to being in love. Playing hard to get by delaying their satisfaction will make them eager for you and put you in a powerful position. It's very sexy and saves you from a broken heart if lust is all they seek. To fulfill an emotional need, you may have an intense desire beyond a requirement for food, money, power, or sex. Waging war against an out-of-balance desire helps you take control and so avoid harm. Lovers of wisdom understand what is good and bad, and direct their power to win the war. You're all-powerful and all-knowing.

Aware that in true love souls are connected, you can test whether you are being manipulated by following your own judgment. You're more easily tempted when you feel insecure, but your fighting spirit is there to protect you from master deceivers.

*Waging war against an out-of-balance desire
helps you take control and so avoid harm.*

Like Maeve, no man can be crowned king without your consent. You do not have to settle for the consolation of lust when love is lacking. Your spirit and personality are the ultimate seduction.

You realize the world is made seductive through advertisements, which make you anxious to buy products or persuade you to buy into political beliefs. All that glitters is not gold and people can tell you anything.

MAEVE'S MESSAGE Someone may be trying to lead you astray for their own benefit, perhaps for your time, support, money, or a sexual relationship. People's minds, souls, and bodies are blended through sex, so choose a partner carefully. Bed-hopping men and women are searching for their lacking masculinity or femininity.

MAEVE'S SPELL FOR SEDUCTION Take two roses and name one you and the other the person you wish to have a relationship with. Bind the stems loosely with red thread, so the heads are not restricted. Put the roses in a vase beside a candle, then light this every night until they fade. Bury the roses or hang them upside down until dried if you wish to keep them. Burn the rest of the candle or bury it.

EVE OF MAY SUPERSTITION Maeve presides over the fertility rites of Beltane (April 30), the Eve of May, when fires are lit outside to celebrate the start of summer on May 1. Traditionally, for fertility, homes would be filled with wild flowers on this day, but you can pick flowers from your backyard or buy them in a store. May- pole dancing represents the interweaving of the sexes around the phallic pole.

Iseult

GODDESS OF PERSEVERANCE

KEYWORDS: Awareness • Duration • Wonderment

COUNTRY OF ORIGIN: Ireland

A clear, divine light is prompting you to head swiftly after your heart's and mind's desire. Your wishes are sure to be achieved since you have connected to the light of heavenly forces, meaning your life is in sync. Magical, divine powers are weaving through you, giving you vitality and capability from a higher plane as tools to help you reach your destiny through your own actions. From out of the blue, as if by magic, miracles are entering your life since you are in tune with divine intervention. You'll see and feel the light energy of spiritual forces linking you to various stages and imbuing you with supernatural radiance. These will appear like stepping stones leading you to your true purpose. Step by step, you will be shown the way and will rise above the everyday sphere to a higher plane that's closer to heaven. The longing of your psyche to speak with heavenly spheres will be granted.

By your own efforts, a turning point in your life has arrived. You'll find yourself mixing easily with a variety of people who will be attracted to your invigorated optimism. You may cross paths with someone significant when you go on a short journey or celebrate an event. Happy days laughing in the sun are forecast.

Feeling physically and mentally bright will reward you with renewed peace of mind and self-belief. You'll easily leave negative people behind who may have held you back or unsettled your equilibrium. The musical vibrations of Iseult's harp are sacred and healing, alluding to you opening your heart to the mysterious source of God and the universe and to connections and coincidences.

During the daytime, while awake, you will be given signs that confirm you are in sync with the light and on the right path. Since you're a visionary, you won't lose the spirit of the light at night. You will receive dreams that predict your future. You may dream of deceased loved ones who give you messages, prophecies, or signs. Other dreams may reveal as yet undiscovered aspects of your psyche, which will empower you to be whole and perhaps take a leap of faith. Your powers of divination are increasing each day, linking you to your powers of truth. Recognize a heaven-sent opportunity by trusting your intuition to see the difference between the profound and the superficial.

Iseult was a skilled physician; likewise, you may be inspired to study herbalism, homoeopathy, or natural remedies for physical and emotional ailments. You're strong-minded. Light will illuminate the path ahead, so you can see your way forward. Obstacles are disappearing, to be left in the past as you move forward. You have wisely avoided being made despondent by setbacks, realizing that they have revealed the strengths you have to survive your ordeals. Perseverance is continuing the arduous work, regardless of the hard work you've already put in. Small steps will get you to where you want to be. You're concentrating on what is necessary and eliminating what is not. You know you will succeed since you persist, are determined, and keep moving forward one step at a time.

ISEULT'S MESSAGE A distressing situation is fading into the past. Small, successive steps will get you to your destination. You're seeing better days and know brighter times lie ahead. Your positive thoughts are attracting love, happiness, and good luck. The heavenly vibration of Iseult's harp shows that you'll attract good fortune when you tune into the higher vibration of positive thinking. By not dwelling on failure, you will attract success. Your thoughts create an aura, an atmosphere around you. Each thought of the same kind further empowers your aura.

ISEULT'S SPELL TO SUCCEED IN AN ENTERPRISE On a Sunday, because the sun governs Sundays, light a yellow, red, or orange candle. Focus on the picture of Iseult. Look at the flame and image for a few moments. Close your eyes and say aloud your desire for your enterprise to succeed. Look at the image again until you are ready to snuff out the candle.

Awen

GODDESS OF INSPIRATION

KEYWORDS: Remembrance • Memory • Illumination

COUNTRY OF ORIGIN: Wales

Awen is the goddess of inspiration and remembrance. A charmer of people's minds, she shows that the essence of life is the flow of spiritual energy. You are oracular, able to foresee events and predict the future for yourself and others. You know you must start a project to achieve the result you want. Now is the time to begin what you've postponed. You'll not achieve as much if you wait to be inspired. You're more capable and braver than you realize. Your social, academic, business, artistic, and creative ideas will flourish. Inspiration comes from within and without, but determination keeps inspiration flowing. Your spirit holds gems of inspiration that are sacred blessings.

Awen's lamp represents the illumination of your inner life. You need to open a door to a higher plane, as shown by the lamp, a symbol of faith, safety, light, intelligence, and protection against the forces of evil. As the wick of Awen's flame is consumed to give light, so you may have to sacrifice your time for a while to concentrate on the project you're being encouraged to begin or finish. A flame can only burn when fueled by a source; you must also cling to what fuels you.

You're capable of doing your best in any circumstances, even when you meet adversity or are out of your comfort zone. You adapt to every aspect of life by not letting thoughts of what you can't do put you off what you can. Even in despair, focus on the light. Inspiration will come and shadows will be left behind, not in front of you. When your wish for something is strong, spiritual powers will support you, as it's your destiny to achieve it. Difficulties will prepare you for miracles to manifest, so keep your inner light burning. Deliverance from someone or something has arrived. You'll be inspired by blessings that awaken your insight and stimulate enthusiasm. Events are in sync with your needs or requests.

Awen's harp strings indicate that your thoughts are being received by a higher vibration, which delivers what you have thought of to you. In a dark situation, you don't lose sight of the light. Look at things from both sides and weigh them up. If you have faith something will work out, you'll see opportunities. You'll see obstacles if you don't believe success will come. If you fear failure, you're not giving your dreams a chance to come true. You will excel if you are committed. Seeing someone, including yourself, win over adversity can inspire you to be strong.

When facing the sun, your shadow is behind you. In winter, it is longer. Your dark days are behind you, are fewer, and you're heading toward the light

Seeing someone, including yourself, win over adversity can inspire you to be strong.

of spring. But you may be at risk of not seeing other people's dark nature, as you're focused on the light, so keep bright to see through them. Don't dwell on other people's bad deeds or listen to those who undermine your ambitions. Instead, mix with people who support and encourage you.

AWEN'S MESSAGE Awen presides over the Fall Equinox (September 21) when there are equal hours of light and dark in the day. You're inspired to take control and become the person you aspire to be. You hold the scales of balance to be victorious over yourself, and achieve your aims. You're more aware of your spiritual strength and this brings you greater understanding with other people. You'll become an inspiration to others when you motivate yourself to make a project happen.

AWEN'S SPELLS FOR INSPIRATION

- Every time you work on a project or your studies, light a votive candle and ask for help. If you're stuck, ask for inspiration to come while you are asleep. You will wake with the answer to how to deal with the hurdle.

- Light a votive candle. Look at the flame and say: *"The flame of inspiration is ignited in me. The light of inspiration is entering my mind, body, and spirit."* Close your eyes and feel light entering you and moving around your body. Open your eyes and gently blow over the flame, so it flickers. You'll feel lighter and inspired. Let the candle burn or blow it out when you feel ready.

Dindraine

GODDESS OF GENEROSITY

KEYWORDS: Excellence • Empathy • Charity

COUNTRY OF ORIGIN: England

A shower of heavenly blessings is being bestowed on you. Everything in life is improving—even what is or has been bad is getting better. Help will grow and become more abundant when you draw it closer to you. You can attract and activate gifts of spirit to work for you when you call for general or specific help. You will recognize the response to your call by people and events sent your way when required, whether for finances, love, legal advice, health, work, or any other situation. You have tapped into an abundant spring, source, or well that will not run dry. A new, well-deserved phase of good fortune in work and love is bringing you optimism and prosperity. You appear to be on a heaven-sent winning streak that brings a surprise bonus or gain your way.

You have a spiritual gift for turning negative situations into positive ones. Able to cope during past troubled times, you remain modest when successful. You channel your abundant gifts to others, even undeserving people, by being generously and anonymously self-sacrificing, kind-hearted, and offering healing without thought of reward, just as Dindraine gave her blood to cure a woman of leprosy. Your generosity is an outward expression of your kindness, making you spiritually

richer. Even smiling and speaking words of comfort demonstrate your generous nature. Your kind words or thoughtful compliments may only take a few seconds to say, but could inspire that person's life forever. You emulate the good qualities of people you know who set a good example.

You show others how to be grateful for what they take for granted, such as two feet and legs and their five senses. You help activate their gifts for hearing spirit speak to their heart, see spiritual interaction through dreams and visions, or have a deep feeling or knowing. Your power of communication flourishes in business, health, and love, confirming your belief in divine intervention. People destined for you are appearing in your life for a good reason. News from an acquaintance or relative will move your life forward, so be alert to introductions and expect good results. An imminent important event will make you feel uplifted. If you're dreading an occasion, it will turn out to be better than you anticipate. The end result will be worth all the effort.

You'll succeed in all matters of the home and heart. You're quietly organized, resourceful, and sparkling with wit. Good news will make a problem look more promising than you hoped. Someone will go out of their way to assist you and also travel to help.

Journeys, study, and new ideas will now benefit you most. Happy events are putting you in touch with good situations fated for you. Your mind is more receptive to deeper levels of your psyche, so anything that feels intuitively right or wrong, is. A love relationship will turn out happily, boosting your self-esteem and status. Someone who loves you and has your best interests at heart will give you a gift to show their appreciation. You're a source of comfort to someone with whom you have a heart-to-heart conversation. For yourself and others, you'll be putting your God-given gifts to good use.

DINDRAINE'S MESSAGE You're a blessing to people, treating them well, perhaps without knowing it. Giving through time, word, gift, or deed reveals you are spiritually kind. It's an outward expression of your spirit and soul being nourished by abundance. A generous personality lasts longer than good looks. You will reap what you sow. Value your time by making the most of, it as seasons change.

DINDRAINE'S SPELL FOR FINANCIAL ABUNDANCE Place a glass of water beside a green or gold votive candle. Put coins in a circle around the candle. Write your financial request on a small piece of paper. Sprinkle drops of water from the glass onto your request and light the candle. Let the candle burn until you're ready to snuff it out. Keep the paper in your purse until your request is fulfilled. Keep the coins in a wallet or purse to spend.

Nimue

GODDESS OF ENCHANTMENT

KEYWORDS: Revelation • Bewitchment • Delight

COUNTRY OF ORIGIN: Wales

Nimue, the Lady of the Lake, was the fairy godmother to Lancelot, one of the Knights of the Round Table. She shows that divine blessings are upon you, too. Nimue offers Arthur the magical sword Excalibur by holding it out of the lake. You'll also be offered a magical tool of protection, whether this is a new love relationship or job, or the means to fulfill a quest. You're assured of success and hold the key to the castles you've been building in the air in your mind's eye.

Like Nimue, you're a goddess of enchantment. People find you fascinating as you lift their spirits by altering their hearts, minds, and actions. Enchantment will come when heaven-sent messages are sent to your heart through people and random signs. As you're a spiritual being in a mortal body, your soul is comprised of reason, spirit, and desire—reasons with a desire, so your spirit rules.

Something miraculous will happen in love or work, as if by chance. What has been hard to do until now will be easy and you'll become the person you aspire to be. Gaining a better understanding of yourself, you will relish life more, worry less, and enjoy a phase of regeneration and rejuvenation.

Your charisma attracts someone's attention and your kind personality wins their heart. A man will fall

in love with you, just as Merlin fell in love with Nimue when he saw her dancing in a forest. Someone already in love with you is seeking a deeper connection. If you have unresolved love issues, you're in a position to calm matters of the heart. Romance will blossom, creating possibilities that fill your heart with love. If you're single, someone is about to aim Cupid's arrow at your heart and could be the love match you've been hoping for. You'll be invited to a social function that could lead to a new romance.

Just as Merlin taught Nimue magic, so you'll encounter divine intervention in big and small ways. It is your destiny to have many enchanted moments, as your heart will hear a spirit voice talking within you or through a person or location. Life is changing since, like a lake, you're reflecting what's on the surface and looking deeper to see what influences your life. Like your image in a calm lake, you can reflect more clearly when you are settled, not upset. Your spiritual journey is recognizing your inner nature. A mirrored reflection reveals only physical appearances, but through mental reflection you'll bring to light the best in yourself. Love that reflected person, as they have been, and will continue to be, with you for your whole life.

What has been hard to do until now will be easy and you'll become the person you aspire to be.

You are making the most of what you have and attaining a personal standard. Allowing your imagination to be limitless brings you closer to success than you realize. The greater your hopes, the better the result. Willing to face challenges with persistence, you will hit your target. You don't lack the knowledge, courage, or willpower to get where you want to be. A time of adversity is behind you. If single, a passionate romance is about to begin. If you're already in a relationship, renewed passion will make it stronger and bring you closer in mind, body, and spirit.

NIMUE'S MESSAGE Nimue reveals magical powers lie deep within you. These are foresight and the wisdom to put your God-given talents to good use. You'll see magical divine intervention putting your life in sync. People destined for you are coming to help your physical well-being and with matters of heart. A time of mysterious blessings lies ahead. You'll visit amazing places and meet life-changing people. There is harmony at home and a reawakening of your creativity.

NIMUE'S ENCHANTMENT SPELL Light a white candle in front of a mirror. Place a dish of water near the candle so they're both reflected in the mirror while keeping the image of Nimue in mind. Push a pin through the candle, so the tip appears on the other side. Look at your reflection, light the candle, and then say your wish aloud. Let the candle burn through the pin, then snuff it out when the time feels right for you. Bury the candle stub and pin.

Kundry
GODDESS OF ENLIGHTENMENT

KEYWORDS: Insight • Awakening • Honesty

COUNTRY OF ORIGIN: Wales

Kundry is bearer of the Holy Grail, a silver cup of enlightenment that King Arthur's Knights of the Round Table went on quests to find. It is thought to be the drinking cup from the Last Supper and to have received Christ's blood during crucifixion. It symbolizes your perfection through spiritual union, as enlightenment brings you inner sight which is superior to physical eyesight. The physical body deteriorates, but the spiritual body is eternal. Blessings from heaven are shining on every area of your life and your cup of happiness will overflow. A proposal, engagement, marriage, birth, or the start of a happy new love life or faithful friendship is being offered to you. Something you've been searching for will be found.

Life is flowing more smoothly now that you're tuning into a daily, weekly, or life purpose and declaring your intention by setting yourself achievable goals. You become enlightened by perceiving and understanding something more deeply—enlightenment is seeing reality instead of illusion, seeing what is true and what is false, and seeing through people (including self-delusion). Instead of allowing others to influence your decisions, you're stronger and more mature, as you're trusting your own reasoning and taking responsibility. With insight you can understand another person's personality, behavior, and motives.

You have good news that you will be excited to tell others. A special occasion is imminent, putting you in a position of divine strength that makes you shine with happiness. This could bring a change of environment. You may begin a new occupation that could be laborious to begin with, but will engage your interest in the future. Your efforts to attain a higher position will not be in vain and may take you abroad. Don't hesitate to take a bold step that will better your happiness. You may become a member of a reputable organization that helps needy people. You're a comfort to many, but more so to one person in particular. A reunion with an absent friend will occur, perhaps someone you feel you've lost sight of forever. Good luck in a speculation is predicted, resulting in a choice of directions which will lead to achievements and success. An easy way to make money may appear, but avoid it at all costs. The right help will come if you stay on the correct path and persevere, and don't abandon a dream due to adversity. Sometimes insight needs to be acted upon instantly, to stop you making a mistake. At other times, your insight will be proved right when you see someone's actions or hear their words.

Realizing a self-delusion, you will be successful if you try to purify yourself from an enemy within or someone who has mistreated you. A fruitless situation should improve if you gather the strength to have another try. A dream can still materialize if you don't abandon it. You will turn creative talents into success. A bonus or well-deserved gain, trophy, or award will be yours. You're blessed with abundant emotional and physical wealth. When you count your blessings you'll realize you have a lot more than you think.

KUNDRY'S MESSAGE The Holy Grail blesses you with powers of enlightenment, happiness, endless prosperity, and eternal life. You're enlightened when your spirit rules your mind and you follow what is right and good. Self-knowledge brings enlightenment, so you can overcome challenges and make life more purposeful. A moment of insight can change your future for better or worse, depending on whether you act upon what your intuition is telling you. Arthur's questing knights were guaranteed self-realization by finding the Holy Grail—so too are you.

KUNDRY'S SPELL FOR FINANCIAL ABUNDANCE
Put three coins in a goblet or glass of water. Place three tealights around the glass. On a piece of gold paper, write in green ink what you want to buy with the money you request. Put the piece of paper face up beneath the glass. Light the candles and let them burn out. Dry the coins and put them in your wallet or purse with the piece of paper. After buying the items you needed the money for, burn or bury the paper.

Eostre

GODDESS OF MORNING

KEYWORDS: Renewal • Rejuvenation • Positivity

COUNTRY OF ORIGIN: England

You are on the threshold of a bright new dawn, represented by Eostre, the goddess of morning and spring. Eostre's name means "Easter" in Old English. You have the power to become who you might be in your imagination and let go of negativity, like a spring flower greeting the daylight as it emerges from the dark earth. You'll change for the better by altering your opinions and beginning each day more happily. Realizing that every morning brings a new start and holds the seeds of how the rest of your day will progress, you'll see opportunities and plan your day to achieve more. Each day is a small life in your whole life.

You're leaving behind what has been a difficult time, ceasing to worry about the past (which cannot be changed) or poisoning your spirit by dwelling on past disappointments. Eostre is a daily reminder that sunshine always returns. A better life is ahead of you, as represented by Eostre's eggs. The eggshell protects an emerging life, which means something you've been preparing for will see the light of day. You'll get the lucky breakthrough you've been working toward. An egg is only positive: being rounded at both ends, it has no beginning nor end, so represents eternal life. You are the artist of your own destiny, able to paint a picture of how you see

your life. You'll start something that needs doing as opposed to waiting for the perfect time to arrive. An overwhelming task can be achieved if it is divided into small daily sections. At night-time you'll look back and be pleased with your renewed vigor and speedy progress.

Good luck and wish fulfillment will come. A new partner is coming into your life if you're single and looking for love. Your relationship will move quickly and could lead to a spring conception, as shown by Eostre's hare, a symbol of sexuality and fertility. If you're already in a relationship, you may soon conceive. Regarding business or property, you'll make fast progress, like the hare that runs quickly and tirelessly uphill. Against overwhelming difficulties you'll reach the top of the hill and look back at your accomplishments. You'll get what you want if you use your day well rather than waste it. Make your day happier by telling yourself each morning that you feel happy. In the morning, smile at yourself in the mirror so your day begins with joy. Every sunrise brings new moments and chances that should not be missed.

Like the morning sun, you rise to spread light on your day and the people around you. You will experience the certainty of faith and miracles by

Eostre is a daily reminder that sunshine always returns.

welcoming fresh challenges. Trust in divine intervention—it may take you to amazing places as Eostre's hare is symbolic of running with God's will. Today could bring your heart's desires. Say every day: *"A miracle will happen today"*—it will and cumulatively life-changing miracles will also occur.

EOSTRE'S MESSAGE Life will be wonderful. A new beginning dawns each day and you've reached a turning point. The dark days are behind you and bright new days lie ahead. If you desire something elusive, do something to get it. Begin each morning willingly and do positive things daily. Keep income and expenditure well-balanced, nourish your inner strength, and love your life.

MORNING SUPERSTITIONS

- Pick up a coin when you see it to bring good luck to your finances and career.
- If you see a coin outside in the morning, which way up is it facing? Heads, you'll get what you're hoping for; tails, there'll be a delay or you won't get it.
- Seeing both the sun and moon in the morning is considered good luck.
- For good luck in an enterprise, walk in a circle in a clockwise direction, starting in the east, before you leave home in the morning.
- For a productive day, get up and watch the sun rise, drawing the light into you. Your inner voice will guide you on what to do that day. If you can't see the sun, light a candle in the east of your room, close your eyes, and listen to the voice.

Rhiannon

GODDESS OF NIGHT AND DREAMS

KEYWORDS: Darkness • Vision • Repose

COUNTRY OF ORIGIN: Wales

Rhiannon, the goddess of prophetic dreams, intimates that your future will be revealed in your dreams. Your soul speaks to you in your dreams while you sleep. Your clairvoyance sees the truth in dreams, so keep aspiring to make them come true. If you believe that they will, amazing things will happen. Dreams also deliver gifts of wisdom and self-knowledge. Your determination and hard work will turn your dreams into reality. Chase your dreams and don't listen to those who accuse you of being a dreamer—your dreams can materialize.

Rhiannon also presides over Yule, the Winter Solstice (December 21), which shows you're on the threshold of better and brighter times. The darkness of night is greeted by a bright new dawn, and you will be too, even during gloomy times. In your darkest moments, there are glimmers of light, just like stars in the night sky. Stars guide you to feel happier and inspire hope in your deepest, darkest hours.

If you're living through a difficult situation, don't let it keep you awake. Not only does sleep reduce stress and replenish the body, but your spirit (which is attached to your body by a silver cord below your navel) also travels to the spirit world. The spirit world feeds your body with energy through the cord. Dwelling on worries before sleep stops your spirit

making this journey. Instead of worrying, say your problems aloud and ask for deliverance from your difficulties. The spirit world will help you, using events that occur through divine intervention in your waking life. The right helpers will cross your path to resolve a predicament.

The spirit world can also help with dilemmas while you sleep. Supernatural dreams will take place, especially when you ask for heavenly help. You can have victory over problems by believing in your dreams and aiming for them with hard work and self-belief, and by taking physical steps to make them come true.

Rhiannon shows you're at a point of change for the better. Your mental and physical equilibrium is in tune with this change. You never lose sight of the light in the darkness. Earthly gifts are coming your way, as are possibly fame and fortune.

Rhiannon's horse alludes to working physically as a team with your spirituality, finding your God-given gifts, and putting them to good use. A project will be greeted by the light of a new dawn, bringing spiritual and financial rewards.

Symbols will appear in your dreams and waking life. These signs are your esoteric knowledge, which will guide you and confirm you're heading in the right direction. Your dreams foretell your future with

your eyes closed. When you open your eyes to your dreams and start living them, your dreams can become reality.

RHIANNON'S MESSAGE The Winter Solstice is the darkest day of the year. Your psychic powers are illuminated while you sleep, enabling you to see your future in your dreams. You can ask for a dream that predicts your future. To do this, before going to sleep, say: *"Please can I be given a dream tonight that predicts my future."* You can also meet loved ones who have passed on if you say: *"Please can I meet [name of person] in my dreams tonight."* If you ask to be healed in your sleep, you will be. The proof will come when you will feel and get better—but don't avoid medical appointments.

RHIANNON'S ASTRAL TRAVEL SPELL Light a silver votive candle in your bedroom. A silver candle symbolizes the astral cord that leaves your body at night to travel to the spirit world. On a piece of white paper, write the name of the person you wish to visit or dream of that night. Put the paper inside your pillow case. While you sleep, your spirit will travel to that person or bring their thoughts to you.

RHIANNON'S DREAM WISH SPELL You can wish for anything, even a new partner, car, job, or home. Light a votive candle in your bedroom. Write your wish on a piece of unused paper. Fold the paper into four and place it in your pillow case. Extinguish the candle before you go to sleep. In the morning, put the paper in your purse until your wish has been fulfilled.

Habetrot

GODDESS OF HEALING

KEYWORDS: Improvement • Restoration • Rebirth

COUNTRY OF ORIGIN: England

Habetrot's wheel, like the Earth rotating the sun, symbolizes your spiritual path through the four seasons of life, in which you spin your own fate. Outside forces, good and bad, impact our fate, but can be interwoven for our benefit when our choices cling to the light. Good times always follow bad ones since the wheel of life keeps on turning. The distaff pole holding the fiber, which becomes thread by spinning, alludes to old age and leaving the wheel of life to ascend to heaven.

All areas of your life are improving, which means everything will go well for you and you'll be thankful for being you. You're experiencing better control over situations and have much success to look forward to. What arrives will leave negativity and sadness in the past. You could make a lot of money in a short space of time and with less effort, obtain your driver's license, buy a new car, or travel far. A love relationship is taking a turn for the better by speedily moving in the direction you would like. Commitment and marriage are predicted. A heaven-on-earth situation is arriving for you because you've been working toward it.

All people who wore clothes spun by Habetrot's yarn were apparently never ill. It is a spiritual cloak of blue light, put on daily from head to foot for protection and spiritual illumination. It works for anyone. Illness is not predicted for you, but if you feel unwell or suffer an injury, keep all medical appointments and your inner wise woman will help you heal. When healing takes time on the spiritual road to physical recovery and emotional wholeness, it allows you to re-evaluate what and who is important. Keeping your sense of humor is healing, music is healing, and being in nature will heal you.

Make yourself do three positive things each day to help overcome depression. Mind over matter works to heal pain. If the healing process takes time, you can still be happy by fueling your mind with positive thoughts. If you're healing from a broken heart or disability, surmount the pain by looking up, not down. Treat your body with respect, as it has to last a long time. By beating what you thought was impossible, you'll gain new strength. If you feel the brakes have been put on your life, keep hopeful—the wheel is still turning. The quiet, slow time can teach you what you're meant to learn and prepare you for good things to come. Facing adversity and being happy each day bring rewards. Your kindness is echoing back to you.

You are good at letting go of the past, and moving onward, realizing that everyone is ruled by the laws

of nature which run through life. Letting things run their natural course brings you a fresh start. You wished matters were easier and now they are. You're about to experience regeneration, good fortune, and a new lease of life. Chances to develop an intelligent area of your life are coming, in which you will prove yourself productive. Kind deeds are greater than kind intentions—don't delay these in case they're too late for others on their wheel of life. Being kind answers another person's prayer.

HABETROT'S MESSAGE Positive things are happening—you're healing and possibly solving a predicament. If you feel you can't alter something, changing your thinking makes it more bearable. Enjoying your life encourages healing on an emotional, spiritual, and physical level. Peace of mind is an option for anyone going through a difficult illness or injury that takes time to pass. Habetrot's spinning wheel is bringing unexpected kindness and miracles, as you keep your eyes on the wheel and never lose the thread of your own destiny.

HABETROT'S HEALING SPELL To heal a situation, bring about a reconciliation, or aid a return to health, light a blue or white candle. Push a pin into an onion, while asking aloud for your situation to be healed. Hold the onion and look at the flame, then close your eyes and imagine blue light coursing through your body, from your toes, up your legs to your spine, arms, and head. Let the candle burn to a stub, then bury it. Keep the onion until it has green shoots, then bury this as well.

Aine

GODDESS OF LOVE

KEYWORDS: Romance • Enjoyment • Procreation

COUNTRY OF ORIGIN: Ireland

Aine, goddess of summer wealth and fertility, presides over the Summer Solstice (June 21). On this day, candles representing sunlight are lit in her honor. Aine increases your chances of winning the love of the one you long for, emotionally, physically, and spiritually. It was believed Aine could shape-shift into a red mare that could run faster than any horse, which means you'll always be versatile and win in love. You're glowing with love-light and many hearts are full of love for you since your heart is in the right place. You'll experience a love life with purpose and meaning and a thrill of love that has no earthly price. If you already have a partner, you'll bring out good qualities in each other. Aine's name means "silver wheel," implying the wheel of fortune has turned in your favor to bring riches and happiness in love. If you've just met someone, the relationship will keep growing.

If you haven't yet met your soul mate, you soon will. As spring and summer blossom, so too will your love life. If you've just fallen in love, the relationship will flourish if you let the other person have the thrill of the chase. You're strong enough to carry love into a higher sphere, rather than have meaningless lovers. You'll recognize a happy change in your love life before it occurs and that feeling will light up a

destiny you didn't know existed. You have many admirers and a sense of your own self-worth. You may receive a gift declaring someone's love for you.

True love has arrived with a person who is sensitive to your needs. Someone wants a relationship with you that will require a leap of faith; you may become engaged or set up home with a lover. If a lover is giving you the cold shoulder to prove a point, it is predicted they will be the first to make contact when you endure the silence or wait for an apology. You'll be in the stronger position when you reunite—Aine was not a desperate woman and, like her, you can bestow or remove a man's power over you. Knockainey Hill, in Ireland, is named after Aine who bit off King Ailill Aloum's ear when he raped her, a revenge that rendered him unable to rule Munster because only a perfect man could.

Youthful love has been romantic for you. To find the strength to begin again when love has failed makes you successful and able to find sweetness in adversity. Love will always find you, even if you don't look for it. The spiritual and emotional wealth of experience you gain may make men feel insecure and revere you, just as the gods revered Aine.

If you've been shocked by infidelity, Aine alludes to the restoration of equilibrium in love. If you ask, heavenly powers will help you meet someone more worthy or put a stop to a partner being unfaithful. Within and without, you have the power to rebalance your relationship. Your love life need not rest on shaky foundations if you call upon higher forces to intercede. Heavenly forces may confirm their intercession by speaking through women you know or via clairaudience (intuitive clear hearing). You might be standing in a queue and overhear a conversation relevant to your dilemma, which reveals the outcome for you, such as: "My brother got back with his girlfriend" or "My sister's got a new partner."

AINE'S MESSAGE Aine symbolizes the highest ideal of female beauty, your own femininity, and feminine intuition. You don't have to be pretty to be beautiful and loved. You have the promise of happiness in love and the flame of love-light within you can never be extinguished.

AINE'S MIDSUMMER SPELL Light a candle on midsummer's day for love-light to come into your life, asking for it to keep your love for life bright.

AINE'S LOVER'S KNOT SPELL Light a candle. Write the name of your current or desired lover on a small piece of white paper and your name on another. Roll both pieces of paper into scrolls and tie together with red ribbon or string and one secure knot. Let the candle burn to a stub. Keep the knotted scrolls in your purse or among your personal possessions.

Turrean

GODDESS OF DIFFICULTIES

KEYWORDS: Arduousness • Hindrance • Dilemma

COUNTRY OF ORIGIN: Ireland

Miracles can develop from difficulties and your expectations will be met in a surprising way. Tribulations bring out the talents you were meant to display. You're good at getting over difficulties, as you've experienced plenty of them. You know that you must not lose spirit and optimism. Challenges are forcing you to move on to a better situation after what has happened. You'll look back with a sense of relief, satisfaction, elation, and freedom when you've surmounted the obstacles testing your personality. You'll realize your strength and feel a sense of achievement when victorious. Your faith supports you through trying times, which you defeat by refusing to give up. Your strong personality and willpower will be revealed to others. The way in which you cope with minor and major difficulties says a lot about the depth of your personality beyond how you appear to others.

There is more than one way to solve a problem. You're wise enough not to repeat an error, as you know that an uncorrected mistake will simply reoccur. If mishaps follow a pattern, you're meant to change the pattern and rescue yourself to avoid further harm and hurdles. This may put you at odds with people who don't like your change of attitude because it doesn't suit them.

Nasty people can teach you a lesson: you're pleased to be you, not them. A jealous, troublesome person might try to stop you getting to where you're meant to be. This person thinks you have something they would like to have. Their jealousy is a self-consuming poison to their spirit and soul. A fairy queen, jealous of Turrean's beauty, cast a spell that turned Turrean into a beautiful caged wolfhound. But Turrean was rescued by her brother. This means the person behind your difficulties will meet a great anticlimax, having recently experienced divorce, unemployment, injury, illness, grief, or death. Your sympathy can help them face their problem head on, do what they must to solve it, and survive. Seeing your loyalty, that person will value you more deeply. In words and deeds they'll show their newfound appreciation of you. You'll be laughing together.

The dog that Turrean was turned into symbolizes fidelity and being faithful to yourself and spiritual beliefs. God is the word dog in reverse and a dog symbolizes all God's qualities: a dog's love is unconditional and they're always faithful, pleased to see you, and nonjudgmental. Difficulties lead to self-development and help you grow closer to God and the beauty of nature and the universe.

Miracles can develop from difficulties and your expectations will be met in a surprising way.

Your inner strength increases when you make up your mind to resolve a problem. Even if you feel you're battling a difficulty alone, you are not. Sincere friends and faithful family will prove their worth and fidelity to you through trying times. When enduring difficulties, keep going and you'll get through them. Don't make life difficult for yourself. Keep it simple.

TURREAN'S MESSAGE You're strong enough not to repeat a mistake, but to use it as an opportunity for success instead. You have an astounding inner strength to overcome challenges. Your endurance defeats obstacles and develops good qualities in you that make the difference between success and failure. Believing you can or can't do something is often a self-fulfilling prophecy. Your resilience grows stronger with a determined effort not to be beaten. Obstacles are often stepping stones that inspire you to do something to arrive somewhere better.

TURREAN'S VICTORY OVER DIFFICULTIES SPELL
Take a white candle, as it represents enlightenment of your soul. Sprinkle a few drops of menthol or eucalyptus oil from the top of the candle to midway, rub the oil in with your fingers, then turn the candle upside down and repeat from the other end. Light the candle and say: *"I banish all negative energy directed at me from [name of person or source] and send it to God to deal with for me."* Sit with the candle or let it burn in a safe place. It can be relit another day. Once the candle has burned down, bury the stub. Repeat the spell regularly until you overcome your hurdles.

Morrigan

GODDESS OF FATE

KEYWORDS: Destiny • Fortune • Lot

COUNTRY OF ORIGIN: Ireland

You are in a good position to direct your own destiny. Fate is sending you many lucky turns of good fortune, uniting you with new friends and acquaintances. You'll meet people who are destined for you and react positively to new, happy, preordained twists of fate. Good fortune will be yours, since you cultivate Lady Luck by thinking in a lucky way and having a bright positive attitude. Through divine design, even misfortune can turn out to be a blessing in disguise and how you perceive an experience can determine your fate. Even when destiny has preordained ill-fate, this can be endured if you make the best of it through free will. If you understand your participation and responsibility, you're less likely to feel like a victim of destiny and more easily able to navigate your way through the episode and life. To improve a situation, push your fate to enhance your life rather than passively wait for a better fate to appear. A catastrophe may be the start of a miracle since fear doesn't stop you making choices that free you from misfortune. While winning, you'll appreciate the good things in life.

Morrigan, the queen of fate and victory in war, is believed to have been a shape-shifter who was able to appear as a crow, which symbolizes birth, death, and mystery. You can also shape-shift by taking action to defeat a weakness within or to change a difficult situation. The result will manifest in improved health, well-being, appearance, environment, prosperity, love life, and relationships.

Morrigan's crow shows you're determined to make changes and never give up. The crow flies straight to its destination and builds a nest in tall trees with a bird's-eye view. This suggests your transformation, versatility, and ability to see things from a higher perspective. A crow's black feathers indicate that you'll have shifts of energy, realize your psychic powers, spread your wings, and soar high above obstacles. You'll experience the living essence and peace of your soul as your situation transforms. You don't have to be stuck where you don't want to be. The destiny of our birth and death is inevitable, but you can get what you want in between. You can't change the past, but you can alter today and yourself by adapting your thoughts and the way you feel, see, think, and believe.

Your destiny is formed by your decisions. Heed your inner voice to help you fulfill your fate by accepting when things are as they are and also avoid ill-fated events. Your inner voice can attract good fortune if you listen to your intuition. You will discover your divinely ordained life plan and know

Your destiny is formed by your decisions.

that providence is smiling upon you. People you love will travel to see you. A long journey, perhaps a deserved vacation, is also predicted for you.

MORRIGAN'S MESSAGE Since your decisions seal your fate, acquire superiority over your destiny by mastering your fate, so things go well, not wrong. Approach those who can help change your circumstances rather than wait for fate to find you. You'll have lucky breaks and create your own luck by making the most of opportunities that come your way. Remember, negative thoughts can repel lucky breaks.

MORRIGAN'S FUTURE PREDICTION SPELL Turn off all electric lights and light a new candle. Stare at the flame, willing it to rise in height or descend. This proves you're in sync with the forces of light and your subconscious mind. Ask the flame questions, telling it to answer "yes" by rising and "no" by descending.

CONTACTING YOUR GUARDIAN ANGEL OF DESTINY AND FATE Light a white or silver candle in front of a mirror. Stare at the flame and look beyond your reflection. The presence you feel or what you see is contact with your guardian angel. You may see the transparent angel's face over your own face or your eyes may look like those of your angel. Ask your angel to show the future. You may see visions in the mirror or hear your angel's voice speak to your mind, so you have a telepathic conversation. You can also say your problems aloud and ask your guardian angel to help you resolve them.

Banba

GODDESS OF PROTECTION

KEYWORDS: Support • Safety • Reinforcement

COUNTRY OF ORIGIN: Ireland

Banba is the protective patron goddess and spirit of Ireland who helps you protect yourself, family, home, and possessions. Banba was also a courageous leader who used magic to ward off enemies and invaders. Your energy will lift, inspiring your faith and self-belief to be a leader. Her contact with the heavens made her strong in the same way that your guardian angels will broaden your peripheral view the more familiar you become with them through practice.

You will hear your angels speak to you. Note what happens when you ask for help with your love or home life, exams, career, finances, sport, health, relatives, or friends. What you see, hear, smell, and feel will confirm the request was heard. You may hear a song that resonates with you and sends a message. You may hear bells ringing or get a ringing in your ears when angels are tuning into you. You may hear a voice prompting you to do something until you take action. You may smell flowers, sent by angels, or colognes you associate with someone who has passed on as a sign they're close. Ask your angel what they're trying to tell you.

Your guardian angels may show you something through shapes and visions in clouds, trees, pools of water, and nature. Watch the shapes evolve and you'll understand the message. Signs can appear in urban spaces as graffiti or on a billboard. In your home or outdoors, angels may appear as orbs (balls of light), or leave a feather to attract your attention and confirm their help and protection. You may experience random synchronicities: see the same numbers or clock time, hear the same words spoken by different people, or hear the same song when it's not often played. If you ask to hear a song, you'll hear it a few days later.

All angelic contact shows you're blessed with love, security, and protection. Banba's name means "unplowed land" and her field indicates you should prepare for change and for new energy to be breathed into life. There is endless potential for you to enter a new field of activity, in love, work, or family matters, where you'll grow physically and spiritually. Germinate seeds in new pastures carefully, so they grow to perfection. Banba shows that you should care for what you value and cultivate yourself.

Prayer is protection, and so are love, family, friends, pets, possessions, and money. Loving yourself, being sensible, and not believing everything you hear are self-defence against outside forces. When things go wrong, this might be protection from a worse situation. Sometimes higher forces keep a person out of your life for your own good, so think twice before chasing after them. New locations and interesting people will make life more varied and educational. New pastures sustain your spirit and body on life's journey. Your self-control and calmness protect you, keeping you happy in any situation and forming a barrier against life's difficulties. Worrying less and living without fear will improve all areas of life. Trust your judgment, as you have the ability to make what you want happen.

BANBA'S MESSAGE Your guardian angels walk beside you. They always protect you, as do loved ones who have passed into the spirit world. Something that you fear may happen, will not. Your angels and own spiritual magic are your most powerful weapons against enemies and there is no obstacle you can't overcome.

BANBA'S SPELL FOR PROTECTION Cut four apples in half. Write on four small pieces of paper: *"Protect me always."* Or, if you have a specific request, write: *"Protect me always from [name of person or thing]."* Conceal one piece of paper between each of the sets of apple halves. Tie the halves together with ribbon or string, then bury them around the base of a healthy tree.

BANBA'S SPELL FOR HOME PROTECTION Sprinkle a few pinches each of garlic skin, dried rose petals, lavender flowerheads, and dried nutmeg into an envelope with your name written on it. Put this under the inside doormat at home. You can also ring a handheld bell in the corner of every room in your home for protection.

Emer

GODDESS OF SELF-ESTEEM

KEYWORDS: Pride • Accomplishment • Confidence

COUNTRY OF ORIGIN: Ireland

You realize that self-esteem and confidence are very good friends. They make you happy, help you value yourself, and create opportunities. Challenges prove you're more resilient than you think. Self-esteem makes life easier to handle and since like attracts like, you'll gravitate toward confident people who appreciate you and make you feel good. You only have to look at someone's actions to see how they feel about you. A person who has passed this test through generosity and helpfulness is coming closer. If single, you may well have met your match.

Valuing self-worth, you will say "no" to one or more people who you've previously said "yes" to. When you keep saying "no," they will eventually accept the answer and this will give you peace and strength.

Once you see that you deserve better, you're unstoppable. Emer, whose name means "swift," knew she was beautiful and intelligent. Valuing her self-worth, she set her suitor Cú Chulainn heroic tasks to show he was worthy of her chastity, femininity, sweet voice, fine speech, beauty, wisdom, and fine needlework. Emer waited for Cú Chulainn to offer marriage to prove that sex without love would steal her dignity—sex after two people have fallen in love is superior, as sexual love nourishes both the body and spirit. After marriage Cú Chulainn had

sex without love with other women, so he and Emer drank a cup of forgetfulness and forgiveness. Gentle, sensitive, feminine Emer was not jealous. With unfailing self-pride and confidence, she knew Cú Chulainn would always return to her.

You're discovering other ways to deal with problems and rise above their uncertainties, increasing your abilities and making your future more secure. You'll feel more light-hearted and loving. Your self-value will grow if you force yourself to do things and replace thoughts of inadequacy with confidence. You know that inaction multiplies fear, but action multiples confidence, which will increase if you're self-assured, even if you don't feel strong. The more you push yourself, the more you'll accomplish at a meeting or event. You will grow bolder in your actions, words, and deeds by focusing on aims, not obstacles, while going after what you deserve in life.

In love or work, you can't force someone to be available, but you're not duty-bound to wait for them to decide when the timing is right. You'll value your time and use it wisely, knowing it's worth loving yourself as much as anyone else. You're more important to people than you may be aware of and will focus on what you've already achieved rather

You're clever enough to be kind to yourself
rather than critical

than on what you have not, so empowering your continuing success. Your faithfulness to your own moral compass enhances your self-assurance, which points you in the right direction for achieving further success. You will thank yourself for something you aim for today, whether it's a tiny daily goal or far-reaching achievement.

EMER'S MESSAGE You're clever enough to be kind to yourself rather than critical. Self-belief makes you more resilient against people with an agenda and you'll have more confidence in your opinions. Don't fear people's judgment when you wish to say "no." If doubt creeps in, illuminate your fears with thoughts of what you can achieve. You'll make the most of yourself and create long-lasting connections and situations. A spark of potential within you can ignite a bright achievement.

EMER'S SPELL FOR HIGHER SELF-ESTEEM Starting at the wick, use a pen to write on a long candle: *"My self-esteem is strong."* Leave an area at the bottom of the candle clear, so the holder does not obscure the words. Smear the candle with menthol oil from the tip and the base to midway. Put the candle in a holder and let it burn through the inscription. Say: *"As this candle flame flickers and burns and the flame rises, so my self-esteem rises."* Let the candle burn through the inscription, then snuff it out or let it burn to a stub. Bury the stub. Look back a week later and you'll see your self-esteem has gone from strength to strength.

Fand

GODDESS OF CHARISMA

KEYWORDS: Attraction • Presence • Appeal

COUNTRY OF ORIGIN: Ireland

Charisma is heavenly spiritual energy. It radiates from your soul, attracting others to you like a magnet due to your spirit-inspired inner light. The enthusiasm you exude due to your divine energy uplifts and energizes others. You bring out good qualities in people, so they become more self-fulfilled and likeable to themselves and others. Outer physical beauty fades with time, but charisma grows through inner contact with the source of the universe.

Fand represents living according to goodness and doing the right thing. This leads to magical happenings due to a synchronicity with divinity. You're about to make a charming first impression. Whether in business or love, a new alliance will soon happen, whether through your own making or spirit working for good, or through someone who wants to enrich your life. An enduring union will develop with that person or with someone that person introduces you to. When you shine with light, people and chances aligned to your soul's progress pursue you.

A family event will strengthen family bonds and blood relationships, as shown by Fand's silver chain of rings linking Heaven and Earth. If a loved one has passed on, you're still connected psychically by the link of love. You'll see the light by receiving a communication from them when you ask for

guidance or a message, developing a two-way bond of communication. Fand can change from a worldly woman to an other-worldly bird, indicating that you can influence the living and the dead. As a bird, Fand is attached to her bird sister by a silver chain. She sympathizes with pain and heartache, advocating healing through correct action. As a woman, Fand has a tear drop on her cheek, representing holy water from emotional springs in your heart, which well up from the source of life within you. Tears soothe, cleanse, heal, and wash your heart's emotions clean by the river of light. You're a flame of light amid someone's dark despair. Fand's name means "weakness and helplessness," but you can rekindle someone's extinguished flame and help them find their way through the dark. Your light is a guiding star.

You know who and what lights up your life and for whom you want to shine. When love radiates through chores and relationships, peace greets you. You'll enjoy self-worth and achievement and move forward to your chosen destination. You'll have fewer struggles and will feel a glow of contentment from trying your best.

Beware of being naive. Although charisma is genuine, charm can be both genuine and ungenuine,

as people can use charm to manipulate others. Focus on the light to avoid being charmed like this.

FAND'S MESSAGE A charismatic event due to divine energy will ignite sparks of joy in you, lighting up your world and those you meet. Bonds of communication formed now will endure like Fand's silver chain. Someone's appreciation will be bestowed upon you. You'll be rewarded for your goodness and for recognizing opportunities in difficulties.

FAND'S SPELL TO ENHANCE CHARISMA Sprinkle a handful of sea salt into a bathtub of running water. Light a candle and take a bath. Look at the flame and ask for its light to cleanse your aura. Put on clean clothes and light a candle in front of a mirror. Turn off the electric light. Sit and look in the mirror while absorbing the light of the flame. This will recharge your inner light and raise your vibration. Put your fingertips and palms together in a prayer position while asking for your charisma to be strengthened. Put your fingertips in the center of your forehead (your "third eye") and ask for light to enter you. Put your hands in the prayer position again and say thank you. Leave the candle to burn safely or snuff it out.

WAYS TO ENHANCE CHARISMA SO YOU EMIT LIGHT Take a walk in nature or stand in a downpour of rain (put on dry clothes afterward). Or walk or sit in sunlight and visualize the light entering your body. Think positively, avoid speaking ill of people, ensure you wear presentable clothes, and keep yourself well-groomed.

Epona

GODDESS OF THE SOUL

KEYWORDS: Spirit • Essence • Sense

COUNTRY OF ORIGIN: Ireland

Your soul is so bright, it can light up a room. You may find your soul mate if you are single or be putting your heart and soul into a relationship or new venture. You have a spiritual and physical relationship with your soul mate. It would be a body-without-soul relationship if it were purely physical. Through the eyes, you can see a person's soul.

You'll love what you're doing and simultaneously feel the presence of spirit (the essence of you as a person). You have, or will find out, what your soul was put on Earth to do. Everything else will fall into place once you've discovered your calling. This may come as a blast of inspiration or be a continuation of what you're already doing that feels intuitively right. Your soul is central to your personality, making you think how you do and influencing the way you look at things, your conscience, and your memory. Your everlasting soul is the non-physical part of you that needs your body. Your spirit can be strong and reliable, lost and found, or derailed and back on track. Choosing good over evil makes your soul stronger.

You're talking to your soul when you're deep in thought. If you listen, you'll hear your soul tell you what to do or which direction to take. Your journey has many paths and you leave one behind to take another forward. You'll find the true path of who you are and will enjoy watching life unfold. In a dilemma, ask and listen to the answers that come to mind. Go with what your heart tells you to do because intuition is a direct message from your soul.

Epona shows that your spirit and body are protected by the Holy Spirit. Her white horse symbolizes your pure powers of divination and victory by elevating you above problems for an easier journey through life. Don't stand still, but gallop through difficulties by dealing with them. Epona's cornucopia suggests there are many earthly and spiritual fruits of prosperity to be enjoyed through the seeds you sow today. Epona's dog means you must keep faith with yourself and your conscience by trusting in God. When in doubt, like a faithful dog, be alert to signs that guide and protect you by warning of invisible dangers. Epona symbolizes your personal security through life and your guide into the spirit world when crossing from life to death. Since resurrection signifies freedom, not bondage, Epona represents getting on your high horse in life and refusing to be belittled. Deal with unfair people, so you're free from dominating constraints.

Be alert like a dog, which can sense what is not yet within sight or hearing. Be faithful to yourself and

Epona shows that your spirit and body are protected by the Holy Spirit.

avoid choices that damage your soul, as a tortured conscience is a soul in hell on Earth. Regrets hurt your soul, which can absorb negativity. Positive thoughts cleanse your soul and clear your mind. Your aura is light emanating from your soul. It must have a source to continue shining and emitting light.

EPONA'S MESSAGE Purity is born in your soul, so you naturally discover what is real and pure in life. Disappointment can be fanned into flame by a beautiful soul shining brightly through it with conscience and virtue. Death is not death, but part of life because your soul never dies. The physical body may fade, but a soul shines more brightly by adhering to good and not letting life corrupt it. You can hear your soul speak, especially when you're alone and quiet for a few minutes, but it can speak to you wherever you are. Be kind to both yourself and others in order to nourish your precious and sensitive soul.

EPONA'S SPELL FOR YOUR SOUL'S DESIRES Light a white candle and write your soul's desires on a small piece of paper. Fold the paper so it fits inside a small, clean jar, then put on the lid. Enjoy sitting with the flame and ask for the light in your soul to keep burning brightly and never be extinguished. Let the candle burn out or snuff it out, then bury the jar, either on the same day or a day or two later. Alternatively, keep the jar among your possessions and add more soul's desires to it.

Blodeuwedd

GODDESS OF TIME

KEYWORDS: Era • Phase • Season

COUNTRY OF ORIGIN: Wales

Blodeuwedd's short life highlights the importance of living life to the full. She is believed to have been born a woman from a flower, symbolizing lost time and facing life without experience. An opportunity is arising for you to begin again with wisdom, move on, and not be held back by living in the past. Blodeuwedd prophecies the certainty of fall following spring and summer, which means that opportunities pass like the seasons. It is important to sow healthy seeds in the present to secure a strong and pleasing future. Your present is within your control. Don't kill time, but use it wisely since it will eventually kill you in the fullness of time, making you simply a part of people's memories of days gone by.

Live in the moment. Carefully consider a person offering you a future now, rather than love a past partner. You're no longer influenced by someone to go along with how they think you should spend your life, which could, in fact, be a waste of your time, not theirs. Now is the moment to leave regrets behind, enjoy the present, move with the time, and plan for the future. This may be a new job or relocation. If you really want something, you'll use time as your tool to work at getting it. There will be a beautiful flowering if you nurture and cultivate your dreams for your ideal future. A past experience with a certain

someone has given you the experience to live your present and future wisely.

A time of fun and leisure with your nearest and dearest lies ahead. You already appreciate that you can lose or gain money, but the time lost with each passing minute can't be regained. The way you use your time makes your life, and says a lot about what you value and who you are. It is very much a reflection of your own self-worth and value—when you value yourself, you value your time.

An ordeal that held you back, put you in limbo, and made time feel as if it was weighing heavily upon you has passed or is almost over. It made you more worldly wise and intelligent. You'll never have a mental collapse and each overwhelming situation has an ending is the message conveyed by the four moon phases symbolized by Blodeuwedd. The four phases, similar to the four seasons, mean time now belongs to you, so keep moving in harmony with the natural tide of life. What you've experienced has prepared you for a bright new phase, especially in comparison to the tribulation you've endured. It has led to a new beginning that will result in a sweet-scented flowering in you. You may set up a new business or embark on a new beginning in another area of life. Now is a good time to put your home and yourself in order to prepare for the carefree times ahead. You need not be afraid to speak up for yourself since you're a goddess of your own mind and time.

Heaven-sent opportunities will appear, in sync with your plans, confirming you're doing the right thing and fulfilling your destiny. A dazzling future is unfolding, illuminating your spring, summer, fall, and winter. Your future is full of fun and includes an abundance of wealth and love.

BLODEUWEDD'S MESSAGE A bright new season full of happiness in the present and promise for future contentment has arrived. You won't squander precious and irreplaceable time. Each minute should be enjoyed. In order to get where you want to be, keep going when you feel it's easier to give up. You have time to put relationships right with the people you appreciate, but not with time-wasters.

BLODEUWEDD'S SPELL FOR A NEW BEGINNING On the night of a full moon, put a glass of spring water on a windowsill where the moon shines through the window. Or, if you don't have a window like this, put the glass on a table in front of a mirror. Say aloud: *"Time is my tool that I shall use well. The results will be there for time to tell."* Write your aims on a piece of paper and leave the glass in place over night. Next morning, pour the water over a plant in your home or use it in the bathtub or shower. Fold the paper into four and keep it among your personal things.

Cyhiraeth

GODDESS OF CHANGE

KEYWORDS: Reorganization • Restyle • Metamorphosis

COUNTRY OF ORIGIN: Wales

Better times are coming, so you'll move from a stagnant situation to a positive one. You may leave your job for a new one—after the interview, it's predicted you'll be offered the job. Cyhiraeth governs streams, indicating you're flowing forward to change your situation and expanding your existence like a flowing river, lake, or stream. Change is essential, as life does not remain rigid, but is constantly changing. Follow your intuition and use your adaptability to go with the flow, and you will alter your situation. You don't fear changing demands since they lead to success. Any predicament can be improved if you fix what's causing it. For example, you can change the way someone treats you by adjusting how you react to them and change your choices by altering your plans. You have the freedom of choice to change your mind and opt for a different future.

Cyhiraeth is said to screech a forewarning against misfortune and death, which means you should change something before you're forced to. The stream of life coursing through your veins improves your health and personality. Like a stream flowing around obstacles, be persistent if you wish to reach your destination without interruption. Rest assured, this change can help you discover your

divine calling. Note that Cyhiraeth is not predicting physical death—she is showing that one stage in life must end for another to begin. Even the most heart-felt desire for change can bring the sadness of leaving a situation behind.

You might change your self-perception, something in your life, or the way you see a person who is bad for you. It may be an inner transformation, from bad to good, which gathers momentum like a stream the farther it travels. By changing direction, you don't have to end up where you don't want to be. Wisely think twice before allowing someone or an opportunity slip through your fingers like water.

Just as Cyhiraeth's horse carries her with speed and vitality, so freedom lies in venturing forward. The end result will be successful if you try further education or a new sport, or start a business venture. Seize the opportunity and don't vacillate.

If you can't change a dilemma, then change yourself. You'll see signs and miracles each day. Good news you've been waiting for will arrive in the next few weeks, helping you move from a frustrating place to one where you'll flourish. You may find happiness in love or your career, or both. Your reward for persevering will have far-reaching

effects for a long time and, like water, will sustain you. Aware of your strengths and weakness, you'll feel pleased with who and where you are.

CYHIRAETH'S MESSAGE Life is endless change and doesn't stop for anyone. Be adaptable to help with unexpected changes and learn from mistakes. You can improve things you want to stay the same as well as those you wish to change. People close by can put you in contact with those who will carry out work you're not skilled at yourself or show you how to do something.

CYHIRAETH'S SPELL TO CHANGE BAD LUCK TO GOOD Find one black and one white object (a black and a white stone, a piece of coal and chalk, a black and a white chess piece, or a black and a white button). Light two white candles and place the black item in front of the left candle and the white item in front of the right one. Sit in front of the candles for a few minutes. Hold the black item in your left hand and the white one in your right hand. Cross your hands and say: *"These bright candle flames are changing misfortune into good and light."* With hands crossed, put the items back in the opposite positions. Let the candles burn down for a while before you snuff them out. Bury the stubs and items (but keep the chess pieces or buttons).

CYHIRAETH'S SPELL TO ATTRACT GOOD LUCK Look into a flowing river or stream and ask for misfortune to flow away and good fortune to flow toward you.

CYHIRAETH'S SPELL TO ATTRACT A GOOD CHANGE OF CIRCUMSTANCES Alter daily routines to a different time or order in which you do them to manifest a positive change.

Bo-Dhu

GODDESS OF NEEDS

KEYWORDS: Abundance • Superiority • Control

COUNTRY OF ORIGIN: Ireland

You are capable of getting what you need. Bo-Dhu, the goddess of needs, shows your needs will be met—her black cow, which symbolizes happiness, nourishment, and abundance, is an omen of this. Her message is to value your needs and not sacrifice them or be misled to please other people. You're not a needy person and others find that attractive. If you can't see what is going on, people will make you feel that your needs are lesser than theirs. Being kind and caring, you're easily manipulated by such people. A lover, partner, neighbor, or friend might make you need something you didn't before, so call a halt when you feel this is necessary. All stages of your life progress, so you'll always have evolving needs and desires. When one need is met, another will arrive.

You attract things that correspond to your vibration by believing you already have what you require. Knowing this, you'll attract what you need to you. The home, job, car, or partner you want is out there—you just need to direct it your way by nourishing your belief that you can get it. A request to the universe can get you what you want and need. It may arrive just as you envisage or in a roundabout way, but you'll still get what you want or require. A lesson and a gift can arrive through what you request by improving a situation for your long-term benefit and finances. You

may want a particular person to do a job, but the one who actually does it will turn out to be better, leading you to other people who'll fulfill other needs of yours. If you have an open mind, you'll see little miracles every day, leading to further happenings that are in sync with your requirements. If you ask for a need to be granted, be ready to say "yes" when it arrives.

New prosperity is coming. Thinking of what you have, rather than what you don't, marks the beginning of attracting what you need. The female power and control symbolized by Bo-Dhu's cow shows that your maternal instincts will also be fulfilled if you're open and gentle. The law of attraction works best when you are receptive and gentle, not angry and aggressive.

Mother Earth knows you require money, a home, and love. When you believe in yourself and feel the universe will take care of your needs, you'll see adversity as an opportunity for the right thing to appear at the right time. In work, a new project will grow and bring you prosperity.

You'll have a loving partner and family. If young and single, marriage and children will happen. If you're not married or divorced, a marriage partner will arrive within months, as you're not destined to be alone. You'll get what you want if you commit to a new start by believing it will happen, whatever has gone before.

The Milky Way, a stream of light in the night sky, is also linked to Bo-Dhu's cow. It shows there is an abundance of things and fertility for your needs, so keep looking up. The Milky Way is regarded as the soul's path to Heaven, but life can be Heaven on Earth for you. You just need to ask for what you want and have faith you'll get it. Aim high, as there is no limit to the wealth and joy you can receive.

BO-DHU'S MESSAGE Ask the cosmos for what you need and it will unfailingly send it to you. You'll use your resources the best you can, bringing abundance through better financial management. You'll have greater peace of mind by buying what you can afford rather than overspending in order to impress other people.

BO-DHU'S SPELL FOR FULFILLMENT The waxing moon will help bring you fulfillment. This is the best time to cast the spell, but you can do it at any time. Write in ink on a piece of white paper a list of what you want or need. Keep it among your personal things. Cut a circle like a full moon from another piece of paper and write the same list on it. Fold this paper in half and half again, then hide it in the hollow of a tree. In time, you'll be able to tick things off your list, as what you asked for will come.

BO-DHU'S CHARM FOR ATTRACTION Doing chores or on the way to or from work, say to yourself: *"I am a magnet for [what you want to attract]. I attract it to me."*

Sequana

GODDESS OF WISHES

KEYWORDS: Desire • Want • Yearning

COUNTRY OF ORIGIN: England

Your wishes are being granted and life is looking brighter for you now. Sequana, a river goddess, shows your life will be a happy voyage of discovery that you will sail through with ease. Good things are flowing your way. Since Sequana's duck-shaped boat is believed to sail in with the April showers, this month will bring unfolding prosperity and valuable possessions that will keep you moving forward like a flowing river. An unpleasant experience will result in something that's very pleasing for you, just as April showers bring flowers to bloom in May.

Sequana, whose name means "fast flowing," is a healer, especially of the eyes, which are symbolic of God's divine providence watching over you. Your clairvoyance and omniscience are opening up and growing stronger. You'll perceive thoughts in your mind's eye that are true and see what is going on around you or being said about you. Sometimes, you only have to work for or speak to someone for a wish come true. Sequana's duck-shaped boat represents you traveling along your spiritual path with faith to wish fulfillment. Her open arms signify divine forces being ready to hear and answer your prayers and wishes.

Keep believing that anything is possible, as your wishes can come true. Your wishes are sent into the cosmos and received. What you need will be provided. You must keep going, just as a river is constantly flowing. A river never flows backward, symbolizing the irreversible passing of time.

Moving forward will help you more than looking back. If you adapt, you'll survive since like a river you have the same force of nature pushing you on to reach your ocean. A new opportunity for achieving your wish is presenting itself, but you should navigate toward it and move swiftly, as it might not wait. In adversity, be adaptable like a duck that can swim, walk, and fly alone or in formation. See your aim, head for it, and you'll get your wish without having to settle for less than you hoped for. You'll find a way of doing what you wish to and people will be valuing you for who you are.

People will be surprised and think you have a magical power to attract what will seem like a miracle. A person is looking lovingly at you and your situation. What transpires will fill you with a sense of optimism that you should welcome with open arms. Your dream partner, family, job, car, or home can be attained. You're going to be celebrating a wedding or the birth of a child. You could also be making an adventurous journey across water.

When your heart is set on a wish, universal energy will help
your wish fulfillment flow your way.

Word your wish carefully, so what you wish for is really what you want. When your wish arrives, it could be that you want more than you wished for as you said: *"All I wish for."*

Your real wish is for happiness, as well as wealth, love, and health. You're aware that money alone doesn't bring complete happiness. If you get richer, you may remember being happier when you had much less and were striving for material things. When you get your wish, you'll feel like an excited child opening presents or looking forward to a vacation.

SEQUANA'S MESSAGE When your heart is set on a wish, universal energy will help your wish fulfillment flow your way. With faith, your conscience and subconscious can work to help the granting of your wish. Some wishes can be fulfilled by your subconscious connecting to your actions. Wishes can arrive instantly or in time. Look out for your wishes and welcome them with open arms when they arrive.

SEQUANA'S SPELL TO MAKE A WISH COME TRUE Find a feather to represent Sequana's duck and put it in the center of a handkerchief. Sprinkle some dried sage (known to promote wishes) and ground allspice (for luck), plus fresh or dried rosemary (for energy) and lavender (for communication). Write your wish or wishes on a small piece of paper and put this on top of the ingredients. Gather the corners of the handkerchief and tie the ingredients into a ball with green ribbon or string. Carry your wishing pouch with you or keep it among your personal possessions.

Nair

GODDESS OF MODESTY

KEYWORDS: Unassuming • Unpretentious • Simplicity

COUNTRY OF ORIGIN: Ireland

A new era is dawning, as Nair symbolizes the turning point of death, rebirth, and fertility. Due to the energy you've invested, you're reaching the end stage of a period of growth and can enjoy the fruits of your hard work. Your plans, even slow-going ones, are coming to fruition. You may have been living frugally, but don't curse the restriction of darkness—you'll see things more clearly if you light a candle and ask the universe for help. You'll enjoy the difficult phase turning into its abundant opposite. Nair's name means "modesty" and it is this trait in you that enables divine happenings to come your way. Others appreciate your modesty when you thank them, as this makes them feel good. Your modesty attracts worthwhile people who can help you create order and achieve your aims. Having a modest, thankful, open heart draws what you need, and are waiting for, to you.

Many earthly treasures are coming, including an increase in wealth. Someone close may surprise you by offering money or something you want at a bargain price. A negative phase, perhaps of financial or emotional hardship, is ending, bringing a fresh start and opening your mind to a new way of thinking. To make progress, try something new that pushes you beyond your comfort zone. You might

start a new job after an academic course. Have no fear regarding a new venture, since Nair symbolizes continued hope for seeds within you to flourish.

The seed of all-knowing in your heart is aware of these forthcoming treasures, so never give up hope or expectation. Just as a seed becomes a nourishing crop over time, so your thoughts put into action will produce results. Seeds nurtured by you can bend around obstacles as they grow toward the light before reaching fruition. Nair is said to have led kings to find treasures when passing from life to death and this alludes to you discovering your fighting spirit. You'll escape a difficult situation by balancing your plans with what your psyche tells you is right, putting you in a superior place. Allow your soul and personality to evolve and move on from entrapment, so you find the treasures within and bring them to the surface to cultivate. Nair also means "learn," so have no regrets in learning. Sustain the deep and best knowledge you have within your soul at the time you make any choice.

A difficult situation is transforming into a happy outcome, so you'll adapt to much better circumstances and bring in a run of good fortune. A major change is coming, based on your previous hard work and determination. Life will seem less

stressful, much sunnier, and more harmonious. You'll
have time to enjoy simple pleasures and luxuries too.
You'll magnify your blessings by appreciating what
you've gone through, what you now have, and the
miracles you can expect to receive.

NAIR'S MESSAGE You'll enjoy more prosperity and
a new lease of life. You'll see the power of good
working for you and count your blessings. Your
talent is a God-given gift; remain modest. You stop
being taken advantage of and adjust the way you
treat those you take for granted. Appreciating the
sincerity to be found in simplicity, you'll nurture your
soul, feel happy with what you have, and be faithful
to your principles. You'll get better at relationships
and finances, work and pleasure.

NAIR'S SPELL FOR FERTILITY IN YOUR PLANS
Light a candle or a votive candle in a safe place.
Keep the image of Nair in mind. Speak to the flame,
as if it is Nair. Explain your problem and how you'd
like it to be solved. In time, you'll find it is solved for
your higher good. Look at the flame for a few
minutes, close your eyes, and ask Nair for visions in
your mind. If what you see is surrounded by light or
a watery edge, you're seeing psychically; if not,
you're seeing your imagination. Either way, you have
channeled a vision of your future. Sit with the candle
or leave it aflame while you do other things—the
energy will keep going upward, so you're
connected to Nair's help. When ready, let the flame
extinguish or snuff it out.

Cethlenn

GODDESS OF PROPHECY

KEYWORDS: Perception • Divination • Predictions

COUNTRY OF ORIGIN: Ireland

The town of Enniskillen, in Northern Ireland, is named after Cethlenn, a prophetess proved right when she forewarned her husband Balor he would be defeated in battle. You also have a supernatural power you can connect to—it is on your side and in control of your circumstances. You can feel satisfied in your soul and secure in the present and future, as you have an inner seed of omniscience. You're foretelling your future, as you're in touch with the divine. Your relationship with the divine won't fail and you'll keep believing, even when your faith is tested.

It is prophesied that miracles will happen in all areas of your life. You'll be delivered from an unpleasant situation, especially if you ask for the patience to trust that divinity knows what's best. Answers to your present and future will come from within as you can see clairvoyantly. You also have the power to interpret signs from without, which you make sense of within. Your gifts for divination will increase, as prophecies will spring to mind without conscious thought. Your gift, protecting you from adversity or ensuring you make the right choices, may help others, too.

Believing in your connection to the divine affects your attitude and actions. To find your spiritual gifts, do something you enjoy, as this talent will help you find that which you feel compelled to do. Having discovered your academic or vocational spiritual gifts, you'll find opportunities opening up to use them. This is because you're in sync with the supernatural and occupying your anointed position. Your destiny is in your own hands and those of the supernatural. You can control your future and handle what comes, as you can choose a different path by changing your mind or attitude. Limitations in your mind become limitless when you use your psyche as this reveals a vision of what you will become or where you'll be.

When you prophesy and predict the future you will be shown an end result. Seeing the end result of a prophecy makes you determined to ensure it is self-fulfilling. You're inspired and imbued with the confidence to make sure your prediction comes true. If your determination is strong, you'll never fail. If the outcome takes time to manifest, keep faith. You were shown the result, but not necessarily how long it might take. This can be beneficial in a situation if you think something is beyond your abilities, but it won't be in the fullness of time. Not having what you want may turn out to be lucky. The work of supernatural forces will always bring you good. You create your fate each day by what you think and do.

Believing in your connection to the divine
affects your attitude and actions.

CETHLENN'S MESSAGE You'll receive psychic messages before the premonition becomes reality. If messages wake you up at night, accept them and don't push the communication away—it might be too late for spirit to give messages further down the line. Or the message could be crucial for that day. By using prophetic tools such as cards, runes, a dowsing pendulum, crystal ball, tea-leaf reading, or messages you receive in your dreams, you'll discover the preferred methods for triggering your clairvoyant gifts.

CETHLENN'S SPELL TO SEE YOUR GUARDIAN ANGEL Light a candle in front of a mirror while keeping the image of Cethlenn in mind. Look at the flame for a few minutes and ask your angel to appear in your mind's eye. Close your eyes and your angel will appear. Telepathically or verbally, ask your angel their name and you'll hear it in your mind. Open your eyes, look at your reflection, and you should see your angel's transparent face on top of yours.

CETHLENN'S DIVINATION TO INCREASE YOUR PSYCHIC POWERS You can give a friend a message, relating to their past, present, or future, and so can they for you. Sit opposite or beside your friend. Light a candle and look at the flame together for a few moments before you both close your eyes. Ask the supreme power of the universe to show you something visually or allow you to sense or hear something about each other. After about five minutes, both of you should open your eyes and say what spirit messages you received for each other.

Index

Adsullata 47–49
Aerten 85–86
Aimend 27–29
Aine 110–111
Andraste 57–59
Anu 40–41
Arianrhod 14–16
Awen 92–94

Ban-Chuideachaidh Moire
  42–44
Banba 118–119
beauty 32–34, 111
Beltane 89
bird omens 25, 34, 86
Blodeuwedd 128–129
Bo-Dhu 133–134
Branwen 25–26
Brigit 22–24

Cailleach 75–76
Caolainn 70–71
Cerridwen 52–54
Cessair 60–61
Cethlenn 140–142
change 130–132
charisma 97, 123–124
childbirth 42
clairvoyance 35–37, 105, 135
Cliodna 32–34
communication 45–46, 95
courage 57, 59, 60–61
Coventina 19–21
Cred 35–37
Cyhiraeth 130–132

Dana 12–13
decision-making 17–18, 47, 82,
  117
difficulties, coping with 112–114
Dindraine 95–96
divination 24, 44, 54, 56, 59,
  76, 90, 140, 142
Druantia 55–56

Elen 17–18
Emer 120–122
emotions 25–26
empowerment 9, 12–13, 19, 90
English goddesses 17–18,
  57–59, 65–66, 72–74,
  77–79, 82–84, 95–96,
  102–104, 107–109, 135–137
Enid 80–81
enlightenment 14, 72, 74,
  100–101
Eostre 102–104
Epona 125–127

Fall Equinox 51, 52, 94
Fand 123–124
fate/destiny 30, 35, 71,
  115–117, 140
fears, combating 12, 13, 30, 50,
  62, 119, 122
fertility 25, 27, 37, 51, 89, 102,
  110
fidelity 22, 56, 67, 69, 81, 112
financial prosperity 40–41, 45,
  50, 72, 96, 101
Flidais 62–64

generosity 95–96
good fortune 14–16, 26, 30,
  40, 52, 66, 72, 74, 102, 115
good health 27–29, 46, 107
gratitude 72–74, 95
guardian angels 117, 118, 119,
  142
Guinevere 67–69

Habetrot 107–109
Hallowe'en 17
happiness 19–21, 45, 72, 77,
  100, 102
healing 107–109
home comforts 22–24, 42

Igraine 77–79
Imbolg 22
inspiration 75, 92–94
intuition 9, 27, 29, 35, 37, 125
Irish goddesses 12–13, 22–29,
  32–37, 40–46, 50–51,
  60–64, 70–71, 87–91,
  110–127, 133–134, 138–142
Iseult 90–91

justice 82–84

kindness 32, 56, 77, 95, 96,
  109
Kundry 100–101

Latiaran 50–51
leaf superstition 56
love 69, 110–111
  see also relationships

love spells 66, 69, 79, 89, 111
loyalty 80-81
Lughnasadh 12, 51

Maeve 87-89
magic and enchantment 50-51,
  54, 97-99
Marcia Proba 82-84
marriage 67-69, 133
miracles 47, 61, 72, 75-76,
  104
modesty 95, 138-139
Modron 37-39
Morgan le Fay 65-66
morning 102-104
morning superstitions 104
Morrigan 115-117
motherhood 37-39

Nair 138-139
needs, valuing and fulfilling
  133-134
New Year 44
night and dreams 27, 90,
  105-106
Nimue 97-99

optimism and positivity 19, 21,
  50, 52, 60, 90, 91

peace 19, 21, 22, 26, 34, 46,
  49, 54, 69, 85-86
perseverance 31, 35, 57, 90-91
prayers 47-49
prophecy 140-142
  see also divination
protection 46, 47, 65, 118-119
pyromancy 24

Ragnall 72-74
rainbows 45, 46

relationships 17, 22, 24, 25, 35,
  42, 50, 57, 60, 62, 65, 66,
  67-69, 72, 77, 87-89, 97,
  102, 110-111, 120
respect and self-respect 19,
  77-79, 80, 81
Rhiannon 105-106
Rosmerta 45-46

Scathach 30-31
Scottish goddesses 19-21,
  30-31, 55-56, 75-76
seduction 87-89
self-belief 32, 52, 65, 90, 105,
  118, 122
self-esteem 49, 96, 120-122
Sequana 135-137
sexuality 25, 87, 89, 102, 120
shooting star omens 71
silence 55-56
sorcery 65-66
soul 16, 25, 32, 60, 82, 97,
  105, 125-127
spells
  to achieve your aim 31
  astral travel 106
  for befriending yourself 54
  for the birth of an ambition 39
  for clairvoyance 36
  for courage 61
  for empowerment 13
  enchantment 99
  to enhance charisma 124
  for financial prosperity 41, 74,
    96, 101
  for fulfilment 134
  for future prediction 117
  for good fortune 16, 26, 132
  for good health 29
  for healing 109
  for inspiration 94

for legal success or justice 84
love spells 66, 69, 79, 89, 111
for a new beginning 129
for a new job 74
prayer spell 49
problem-solving 18, 21, 31, 59,
  139
for protection 119
for reconciliation 86
to see your guardian angel 142
for self-esteem 122
for soul's desires 127
for success in an enterprise 91
for travel 64
for victory over difficulties 114
wishing spells 26, 51, 59, 81,
  106, 137
sports and hobbies 17-18, 19,
  50-51
Spring Equinox 30

time 128-129
travel 27, 62-64, 80, 106, 117
truth 52-54, 105
Turrean 112-114

victory 17, 30, 51, 57-59, 114

Welsh goddesses 14-16,
  37-39, 47-49, 52-54,
  67-69, 80-81, 85-86,
  92-94, 97-101, 105-106,
  128-132
Winter Solstice 105, 106
wisdom 30, 57, 60, 70-71, 75,
  105
wishes 135-137
wishing spells 26, 51, 59, 81,
  106, 137

youth 42, 44